DELICIOUS DISNEY

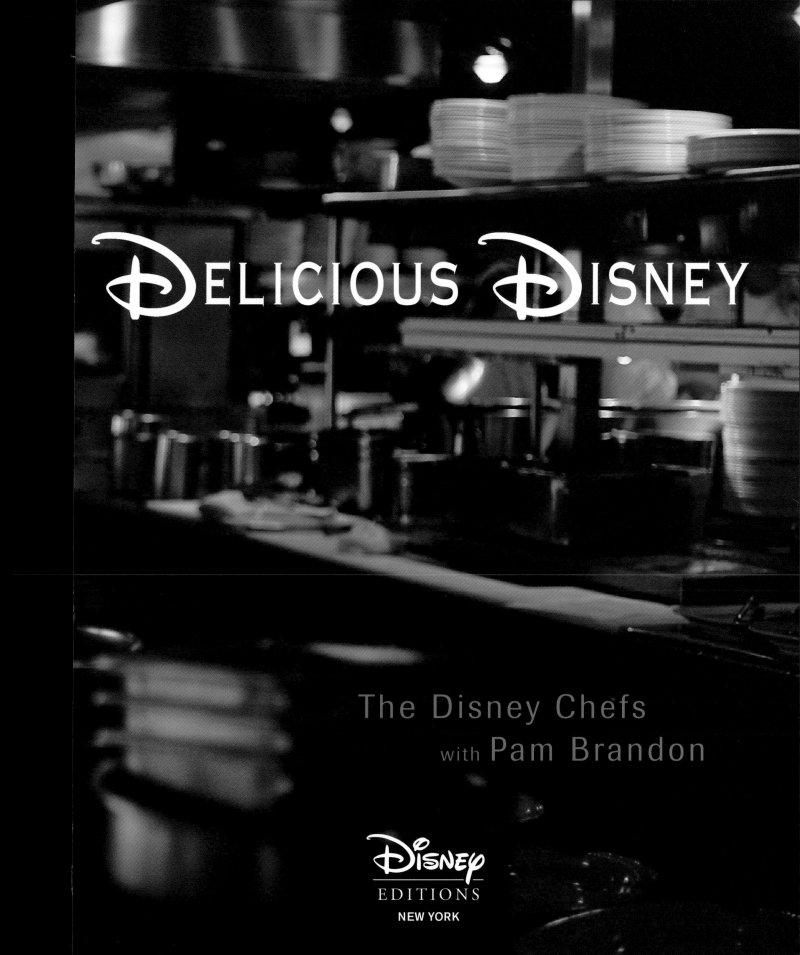

DELICIOUS DISNEY

The Disney Chefs
with Pam Brandon

Disney
EDITIONS
NEW YORK

FOREWORD

DISNEY'S WELL-TRAVELED GUESTS know more than ever about food and wine. They want more choices, better service, more convenience, new taste sensations.

Their sophistication is no surprise, as restaurant-based reality TV has made truffle oil and balsamic vinegar the ketchup and chili sauce of our age. TV chefs are entertaining viewers with trends, products, regional cooking, green markets, exotic travel destinations, and kitchen tools. The Internet has made it possible for those who can't boil water to order gourmet meals that go from the freezer to the table in 10 minutes.

Leading, not following, is our direction. Diets du jour, fads, and the needs of health-conscious guests are part of our daily life. The talented, diverse Disney chefs are highly knowledgeable about food, but also like to have fun in the kitchen—and share that joy with our guests.

But great food is only half the story. We've stepped up wine service, too, and educate all restaurant staffers about wine. Today we have nearly 300 sommeliers at Walt Disney World Resort and more than 200 at the Disneyland Resort. We have come a long way!

As a team, we continue to learn and practice the basics of great cooking, baking, service, and hospitality. And we strive for simplicity in cooking and food preparation through attention to detail. The quality of the food experience combined with great service is the foundation to building long-lasting relationships with our guests.

This book is a true representation of the many, many recipes that diners request, and is driven by guest preference, not professionals, with recipes meant to elicit wonderful vacation memories of another time and place.

The Disney dining experience is an important part of the company's evolution. We hope to continue the momentum, and to always exceed your highest expectations.

—Dieter Hannig
Senior Vice President
Walt Disney World Food & Beverage

INTRODUCTION

A FINE MEAL is such a delightful vacation diversion. I remember my first taste of ethereal Stilton cheesecake with a vintage port at Victoria & Albert's, but just as fondly I recall the old-fashioned cheeseburger and chocolate malt with my kids at Beaches & Cream Soda Shop. Good food is a part of our memories.

For Disney, it is a real balancing act to offer something for every palate, with cuisine as varied as the millions of guests from around the globe. So in this cook-friendly book we have included a little bit of everything too, with recipes that make it easy to enjoy the dishes at home. Some are fuss free. Others take a little time. It's a diverse collection of the best of the best, of good times shared over meals.

In more than 50 years of Disney theme parks, menus have changed with the seasons and with the times, and many of the recipes reflect the trends. Savory dishes like Spoodles' lemon-garlic shrimp or the Germany Biergarten's crisp potato pancakes with smoked salmon are sure to be crowd-pleasers. You can go over the top with the Portobello Cappuccino Bisque from Napa Rose. A dense peanut butter cake from *Disney Cruise Line* provides a rich ending to a grand dinner. For an indulgent breakfast, whip up the French toast with mascarpone cream from Tony's Town Square in the *Magic Kingdom*.

No collection of favorites would be complete without dishes that have never left the menu, like the audacious Tonga Toast at *Disney's Polynesian Resort*, or Disneyland's indulgent Monte Cristo. They are here in the Classics chapter.

The Disney chefs are a talented and amiable bunch, and it was a delight to work with them, sifting through hundreds of their dishes to choose the very best, testing and downsizing recipes that serve hundreds to portions for just six or eight. We think this collection will delight the whole family, and hope that you will enjoy creating a memory of a favorite Disney dining experience.

—Pam Brandon

TABLEC

FCONTENTS

RECOLLECTIONS OF VACATION often come back to food—to a special dinner eaten elbow to elbow with family and friends. Classics like a delicate Stilton Cheesecake at Victoria & Albert's; Sonoma Goat Cheese Ravioli savored with a view of the Magic Kingdom fireworks at California Grill; knockout Crab Cakes at Flying Fish Cafe on Disney's BoardWalk; *a light-as-air*

DISNEY CLASSICS

Chocolate Soufflé at Palo on the

Disney Magic® ship. *Re-create your favorites for a special celebration, or please the kids with a big platter of Tonga Toast for a weekend breakfast, or a stack of decadent Monte Cristo sandwiches for a Saturday lunch. Whatever your idea of an inspired get-together, these longtime favorites are irresistible.*

Maple Glazed Salmon
with Onion-Mashed Potatoes

ANIMATOR'S PALATE ❋ DISNEY CRUISE LINE

SERVES 4

Maple Glaze

¼ cup brandy

1¼ cups maple syrup

1 tablespoon cornstarch mixed
with 2 tablespoons water

1. Pour brandy in a pan and flambé for 5 seconds.

2. Add the syrup and heat.

3. Whisk in the cornstarch and water mixture, and simmer
   for 5 minutes, stirring. Cool to room temperature.

Onion-Mashed Potatoes

2 medium onions,
roughly chopped

2 tablespoons olive oil

2 pounds red potatoes

⅔ cup milk, warmed

2 tablespoons unsalted butter

Coarse salt and freshly ground
white pepper, to taste

1. Preheat oven to 375°F.

2. Toss the chopped onions with olive oil and bake for
   15 minutes, until soft. Purée onions in a blender.

3. Cover potatoes with water in a medium saucepan and boil
   until tender when pierced with a fork.

4. Put drained, warm potatoes in a mixing bowl. Add milk and
   butter, and mash with an old-fashioned potato masher.
   Season to taste.

Salmon

4 salmon fillets, 7 ounces each

2 tablespoons olive oil

Coarse salt and freshly ground
black pepper, to taste

Diced red peppers,
for garnish (optional)

1. Preheat oven to 350°F.

2. Brush the salmon with olive oil and season with coarse salt.
   In a preheated sauté pan, sear both sides.

3.   Place on a baking sheet and drizzle 1 tablespoon of the maple glaze on each salmon fillet. Bake 12–15 minutes, or until desired doneness.

4.   To serve, top potatoes with salmon and drizzle with remaining maple glaze. Top with diced red peppers and minced scallion, if desired.

WHAT TO DRINK: Hartford Pinot Noir, Sonoma. The bright cherry flavors and silky texture match the richness of the salmon.

Sonoma Goat Cheese Ravioli

CALIFORNIA GRILL ✳ DISNEY'S CONTEMPORARY RESORT

✳ WALT DISNEY WORLD RESORT

SERVES 4 TO 6

1 pound soft mild goat cheese, crumbled

5½ ounces aged goat cheese, crumbled

½ cup seasoned bread crumbs

2 tablespoons store-bought basil pesto

2 teaspoons extra-virgin olive oil

2 teaspoons Roasted Garlic Purée (*recipe follows*)

½ teaspoon salt, or to taste

⅛ teaspoon freshly ground pepper, or to taste

16 egg roll wrappers

1 large egg and 1 tablespoon water for egg wash

Clear Tomato Broth, optional (*recipe follows*)

1. In a large bowl, stir together the mild goat cheese, aged goat cheese, bread crumbs, pesto, olive oil, roasted garlic purée, salt, and pepper until well combined.

2. On a work surface, lay out 8 egg roll wrappers and brush each with the egg wash. With a sharp knife, mark each wrapper into 4 squares, taking care not to cut all of the way through. Place about 1 tablespoon of the goat cheese mixture in the center of each square. Cover with the 8 remaining egg roll wrappers and press the edges together.

3. With a knife, cut each double wrapper with filling into 4 squares, to yield 32 squares of filled ravioli. Press the edges together. (If you are not using the ravioli immediately, sprinkle them lightly with cornmeal and store refrigerated between layers of waxed paper.)

4. When ready to serve, cook the ravioli in a large pot of boiling salted water for 1 to 2 minutes. Drain completely.

5. Serve with clear tomato broth, if desired.

(continued)

Cooks' notes: If you don't want to make the tomato broth, top the ravioli with chopped, seeded ripe tomatoes—or a tomato juice "cocktail" also makes a suitable broth.

Clear Tomato Broth

MAKES 4 CUPS

15 whole vine-ripened tomatoes

1 teaspoon salt

1. In a blender, in batches, coarsely chop the tomatoes with the salt.

2. Place the chopped tomatoes in a large sieve lined with a double layer of damp cheesecloth, set it over a bowl, and let the mixture drain in the refrigerator for 24 hours to collect the liquid. Discard the tomato pulp and reserve the liquid.

Roasted Garlic Purée

MAKES 2 TABLESPOONS

1 whole head garlic

1 tablespoon olive oil

1. Preheat oven to 400°F.

2. Cut off the stem and top third of 1 whole garlic head.

3. Place the garlic on a sheet of heavy-duty aluminum foil and drizzle with olive oil.

4. Wrap the garlic with foil, seal the edges tightly, and roast for 1 hour.

5. Remove the package from the oven, open carefully, and let the garlic cool slightly.

6. Scrape or squeeze the pulp from the garlic cloves.

WHAT TO DRINK: Sauvignon blanc is a classic match with goat cheese, and Mason Sauvignon Blanc from Napa Valley has the structure and acidity to nicely complement this dish.

Canadian Cheddar Cheese Soup

SERVES 10

1. In a 4- or 5-quart Dutch oven, cook the bacon, stirring, over medium heat for about 5 minutes, or until lightly browned.

2. Add the red onion, celery, and butter and sauté for about 5 minutes, or until the onion has softened.

3. Add the flour and cook, stirring constantly, for about 4 minutes over medium heat. Whisk in the chicken stock and bring to a boil for 1 minute. Reduce heat to a simmer and cook for 15 minutes, stirring occasionally.

4. Add the milk and continue to simmer for 15 minutes. Do not boil after you add the milk.

5. Remove from the heat and stir in the cheese, Tabasco sauce, Worcestershire sauce, salt, and pepper until the cheese is melted and the soup is smooth. Stir in warm beer. If the soup is too thick, thin with some warm milk.

6. Serve the soup hot, garnished with chopped scallions or chives.

WHAT TO DRINK: Although a hearty Canadian ale works, Jackson-Triggs Merlot, Okanagan Valley complements the rich flavors.

½ pound bacon, cut into ½-inch pieces

1 medium red onion, cut into ¼-inch pieces

3 celery ribs, cut into ¼-inch pieces

4 tablespoons butter

1 cup all-purpose flour

3 cups chicken stock

4 cups milk

1 pound white cheddar cheese, grated

1 tablespoon Tabasco sauce

1 tablespoon Worcestershire sauce

Coarse salt and freshly ground pepper, to taste

½ cup warm beer

Chopped scallions or chives, for garnish

Chocolate Soufflé

PALO ❋ DISNEY CRUISE LINE

SERVES 6

1. Preheat oven to 350°F. Set a full kettle of water on to boil.

2. Butter 6 4-ounce soufflé cups and coat with sugar; set aside.

3. Bring the milk to a boil in a small saucepan. Meanwhile, melt the butter in a medium saucepan over medium heat. Add the flour and cocoa to the butter and beat with a whisk to a smooth, pastelike consistency. Reduce heat and cook for 1 minute.

4. Slowly add the hot milk, whisking until smooth, then blend in melted chocolate. Let cool for 5 minutes, then stir in egg yolks.

5. Beat egg whites in a separate bowl until frothy. Slowly add sugar, 1 tablespoon at a time, until stiff, glossy peaks form. Stir a heaping spoonful of egg whites into the chocolate, then fold in the remaining whites just until combined.

6. Pour the batter into prepared soufflé cups. Place cups in a large baking dish and add enough boiling water to reach halfway up the sides of the soufflé cups.

7. Bake for 20 minutes. Serve immediately, with warm vanilla sauce.

3 tablespoons butter, plus more for buttering soufflé cups

6 tablespoons sugar, plus more for dusting soufflé cups

1 cup milk

3 tablespoons all-purpose flour

3 tablespoons Dutch-processed cocoa

2 ounces semisweet or bittersweet chocolate, melted

4 eggs, separated

Vanilla Sauce (*recipe follows*)

Vanilla Sauce

1. Bring cream and vanilla bean to a low boil in a saucepan over medium heat.

2. Combine sugar and egg yolks.

3. Add 2 spoonfuls of boiling cream to egg mixture and stir well, then pour back into the remaining cream and continue to cook over low heat for 3 to 4 minutes, stirring constantly.

1¼ cups heavy cream

¼ vanilla bean, split lengthwise

3 tablespoons sugar

2 small egg yolks

WHAT TO DRINK: Pour Banfi Rose Regale Brachetto d'Acqui, a sweet and floral sparkling wine that shines with fresh raspberries and strawberries, an amazing complement to chocolate.

Crab Cakes

MAKES 28 SMALL CRAB CAKES

6 cups soft fresh
bread crumbs, divided

1 pound lump crabmeat,
picked over

½ cup finely chopped red onion

½ cup *each* finely chopped
red and green bell pepper

½ cup finely chopped scallions

½ cup mayonnaise

1 poblano chili, trimmed,
seeded, and minced

4 large egg yolks

2 tablespoons fresh lemon juice

1 tablespoon chopped fresh parsley

1¾ teaspoons coarse salt, divided

1¼ teaspoons freshly ground
pepper, divided

⅛ teaspoon cayenne pepper,
or to taste

1 cup all-purpose flour

5 large eggs

½ cup vegetable oil, for frying

Chili Rémoulade (*recipe follows*)

1. In a large bowl, stir together 2 cups of the bread crumbs, the crabmeat, red onions, red and green bell pepper, scallions, mayonnaise, poblano chili, egg yolks, lemon juice, parsley, ¾ teaspoon salt, ¼ teaspoon freshly ground pepper, and cayenne pepper.

2. Form 28 crab cakes, using about 2 tablespoons crab mixture for each, shaping to about 1½ inches in diameter.

3. On a plate, stir together the flour and the remaining 1 teaspoon salt and 1 teaspoon pepper. In a shallow bowl, with a fork, lightly beat the eggs. Place the remaining bread crumbs on a plate.

4. Dip each crab cake into the flour, shaking off the excess, then into egg, shaking off the excess, and finally into the bread crumbs, shaking off the excess. Place the crab cakes on a wire rack.

5. In a 12-inch skillet, heat ¼ cup of the vegetable oil over medium-high heat until hot but not smoking. Add the crab cakes, in batches, and cook for 3 to 4 minutes on each side, or until browned and crisp. As the crab cakes are cooked, remove them with a slotted spoon and drain on paper towels; keep warm. Repeat to cook the remaining crab cakes, adding more oil as necessary.

6. Serve hot with the chili rémoulade.

Chili Rémoulade

MAKES 2 CUPS

1. In a small bowl, combine the chili powder with the water
    and let stand for 10 minutes.

2. In a mixing bowl, combine the chili mixture with the
    mayonnaise, red onion, dill pickles, capers, parsley, tarragon,
    chives, lemon juice, salt, and cayenne pepper.

3. Use immediately or store, covered and chilled, for up to
    1 week.

COOKS' NOTES: These smaller size crab cakes are perfect for
nibbling before a meal. If you'd rather serve them as the main course,
just make the crab cakes larger. You'll be able to serve 4 to 6.

WHAT TO DRINK: The crisp peach flavors with bright citrus
components of Eroica Riesling from Washington State are a
perfect match.

2 teaspoons chili powder,
preferably ancho

2 teaspoons water

1½ cups mayonnaise

¼ cup finely chopped red onion

¼ cup finely chopped dill pickles

2 tablespoons drained
capers, chopped

2 tablespoons finely chopped
flat-leaf parsley

2 tablespoons finely chopped
fresh tarragon

2 tablespoons snipped fresh chives

2 tablespoons fresh lemon juice

¼ teaspoon coarse salt, or to taste

¼ teaspoon cayenne pepper,
or to taste

Stilton Cheesecake

VICTORIA & ALBERT'S ✳ *DISNEY'S GRAND FLORIDIAN RESORT & SPA*
✳ WALT DISNEY WORLD RESORT

MAKES 2 LARGE CHEESECAKES OR 24 2-OUNCE CHEESECAKES

Shortbread Crust

2½ cups all-purpose flour

½ cup sugar

1 cup (2 sticks) butter,
softened, cut into small pieces

1. Preheat oven to 350°F.

2. Blend together the flour and sugar.

3. Add the butter and blend until mixture resembles coarse meal
    (it will not form a dough).

4. Transfer to a buttered 9½-inch springform pan and spread evenly into bottom.

5. Bake for 9 to 12 minutes on the middle rack of oven until pale golden.

6. Cool in pan on a wire rack.

Filling

1. Beat together the crumbled Stilton, cream cheese, and sugar in a large bowl with mixer on low speed.

2. Beat in eggs one at a time, beating well after each addition. Add flour.

3. Beat in sour cream and vanilla until just blended.

4. Pour filling over cooled crust in springform pan.

5. Bake cheesecake for 30 to 35 minutes in a water bath in the middle of oven until puffed and pale gold around the edge.

6. Transfer cake to a wire rack and run a knife around edge of pan to loosen. Cool completely, about 2 hours.

7. Chill covered, until cold, at least 4 hours, before serving.

WHAT TO DRINK: Sweet Royal Tokaji Wine Company Tokaji Aszu 5 Puttonyos from Hungary has a rich texture of apricots, figs, and honey, with natural high acidity that complements the rich flavors of this savory creation.

¾ cup Stilton cheese, rind discarded and cheese crumbled

2½ cups cream cheese, softened

¾ cup sugar

3 large eggs

¼ cup all-purpose flour

¾ cup plus ½ tablespoon sour cream

2 teaspoons vanilla extract

Tonga Toast

SERVES 4

1 cup sugar

2 teaspoons cinnamon

1 loaf sourdough bread
(8 inches long)

2 bananas, peeled

1 quart canola oil, for frying

1. Mix the sugar and cinnamon with a fork until thoroughly blended. Set aside.

2. Slice the bread into four 2-inch–thick slices.

3. Cut each banana in half crosswise, then each piece lengthwise.

4. Place a bread slice flat on the counter and tear out just enough from the middle (do not tear all the way through) to stuff half a banana into; repeat with each bread slice.

5. In a large pot or a deep fryer, heat the oil to 350°F; use a candy thermometer to make certain the oil does not get any hotter, or it will burn.

6. Gently place one bread slice into the oil for 1 minute or until light brown.

7. Turn and fry for another minute on the other side.

8. Remove bread from the pot and toss it in the sugar and cinnamon mixture.

9. Repeat for each piece.

Artist Point Berry Cobbler

SERVES 6 TO 8

1½ cups all-purpose flour

½ cup granulated sugar

2 teaspoons baking powder

½ teaspoon salt

½ cup (1 stick) plus
2 tablespoons cold butter,
cut into small pieces

1 large egg

1 cup heavy cream

12 ounces fresh blueberries

2 tablespoons
light brown sugar

½ pint *each* fresh raspberries
and blackberries, and
8 strawberries, for garnish

1. In a medium bowl, whisk together the flour, granulated sugar, baking powder, and salt. With a pastry blender, two knives used scissor-style, or your hands, blend in ½ cup butter until crumbly. With a fork, stir in the egg and mix just enough to blend. Add heavy cream and mix just enough to incorporate; do not overmix.

2. Preheat oven to 350°F. Lightly grease a 9-inch round cake pan, line the bottom with waxed paper, and grease the paper.

3. Press the dough evenly into the bottom of the cake pan. Place the blueberries on top of the dough and sprinkle with the brown sugar. Place the remaining 2 tablespoons butter pieces over berries.

4. Bake for 20 to 25 minutes, or until golden brown. Cool on a wire rack. Remove the cake from the pan, cut it in wedges, and serve with the fresh raspberries, blackberries, and strawberries. Top with vanilla ice cream.

COOKS' NOTES: Fruit sorbets can be substituted for vanilla ice cream. And you can use any seasonal fruit.

WHAT TO DRINK: Try a sweet wine like Quady Elysium (black muscat) from California, with floral notes of black fruits and vanilla spice, which go well with the fresh berries.

Choux Fritters

MAKES 3 DOZEN

1. In a saucepan over medium heat, combine butter, boiling water, flour, and salt. Beat vigorously until mixture leaves side of pan and forms a ball. Remove from heat and cool slightly.

2. Spoon into a bowl or food processor with a steel blade. Add eggs 1 at a time, beating well after each addition. When all the eggs have been added, moisture should hold its shape in a spoon.

3. In a deep pan, heat oil to 375°F. Dip a tablespoon first in hot oil, then in batter. Carefully drop a tablespoon of hot batter into the oil and cook until brown. Smaller fritters will take about 2 to 3 minutes.

4. Remove with slotted spoon and drain on paper towels.

5. Sprinkle with confectioners' sugar and serve hot.

½ cup (1 stick) butter

1 cup boiling water

1 cup all-purpose flour, sifted

½ teaspoon salt

4 eggs

4 cups vegetable oil, for frying

Confectioners' sugar

Monte Cristo

SERVES 4

1 egg

1¾ cups plus 2 tablespoons water

1¾ cups all-purpose flour

¼ teaspoon salt

1 teaspoon baking powder

8 slices egg bread (challah works well), sliced ½ inch thick

8 thin slices ham

8 thin slices turkey

8 thin slices Swiss cheese

3 cups canola oil

Confectioners' sugar

Blackberry preserves

1. Line a cookie sheet with paper towels; set aside.

2. Whisk the egg and water together in a mixing bowl. Add flour, salt, and baking powder and whisk thoroughly for 2 to 3 minutes, or until smooth, scraping side of bowl.

3. On one slice of bread, arrange 2 slices of ham, turkey, and cheese, covering the bread evenly. Place another slice of bread on top and slice each sandwich in half diagonally.

4. Heat oil to between 365°F and 375°F in a 10-inch pan. Do not let the oil reach a higher temperature than this; if the oil starts to smoke, turn the heat down. Dip half of the sandwich into the batter, allowing excess to drain, and very carefully place into the oil.

5. Repeat with the other sandwich half. Cook 3 minutes on each side, or until golden brown. Place the cooked sandwich on the prepared cookie sheet in a warm oven until ready to serve. Repeat with the other three sandwiches. Cook one at a time, and allow the oil to reach the desired temperature between each.

6. Sprinkle with confectioners' sugar, and serve with blackberry preserves on the side.

New England Pot Roast

SERVES 6

1. Preheat oven to 350°F.

2. Heat ¼ cup oil in a heavy ovenproof pan. Salt and pepper roast, then brown the meat on all sides. Do not let it scorch.

3. Remove the meat and add butter to pan. After the butter has melted, add carrots, celery, onion, garlic, and fresh thyme. Sauté until vegetables are tender. Stir in the flour, and continue cooking until flour is lightly browned.

4. Stir in burgundy wine and beef broth. Add the meat back into the pan.

5. Cover and bake for 40 minutes to 1 hour, or until meat is fork-tender.

WHAT TO DRINK: A great match with this Yankee favorite is St. Francis Merlot, Sonoma, with ripe blackberry fruits framed with vanilla oak and soft, fleshy tannins.

¼ cup vegetable oil

Coarse salt and freshly ground pepper

3-pound boneless beef shoulder roast

½ cup butter (1 stick)

2 cups roughly chopped carrots

2 cups large sliced celery

2 cups large diced onion

¼ cup chopped garlic

2 tablespoons chopped fresh thyme

1 cup all-purpose flour

1 cup burgundy wine

6 cups beef broth

Grapefruit Cake
with Cream Cheese Frosting

SERVES 8

1½ cups sifted cake flour

¾ cup granulated sugar

1½ teaspoons baking powder

½ teaspoon salt

3 large eggs, separated

¼ cup vegetable oil

¼ cup water

3 tablespoons grapefruit juice

½ teaspoon finely grated lemon zest

¼ teaspoon cream of tartar

Cream Cheese Frosting
(*recipe follows*)

1 can (16 ounces) grapefruit sections, drained well

1. Preheat oven to 350°F. Lightly grease a 9-inch round cake pan. Line the bottom of the pan with waxed paper and lightly grease the paper.

2. In a large bowl, sift together the cake flour, sugar, baking powder, and salt.

3. In a medium bowl, whisk together the egg yolks, oil, water, grapefruit juice, and lemon zest until smooth. Whisk in the flour mixture.

4. In a medium bowl, using an electric mixer, beat the egg whites and the cream of tartar just until stiff peaks form. With a rubber spatula, gently fold the egg whites into the yolk mixture until just blended. Pour into the prepared pan.

5. Bake for 25 to 30 minutes, or until the cake springs back when touched lightly in the center. Invert the cake, still in the pan, and cool on a wire rack.

6. Run a spatula or a table knife around the edge of the cake. Carefully remove the cake from the pan. With a serrated knife, cut cake horizontally into 4 thin, even slices.

7. Spread the cream cheese frosting on each layer as they are stacked. Frost the top and sides.

8. Serve the cake garnished with grapefruit sections.

Cream Cheese Frosting

1. In a medium bowl, using an electric mixer, beat the cream cheese on high speed until light and fluffy.

2. Add the lemon juice and the lemon zest. Gradually add the confectioners' sugar and beat until well blended. Add the food coloring, if desired.

WHAT TO DRINK: The delicate sweet peach and orange peel flavors of Michele Chiario Nivole Moscato, Piedmont, will provide a refreshing accompaniment to this Derby classic.

2 packages (8 ounces each) cream cheese, softened

1 teaspoon fresh lemon juice

1 teaspoon finely grated lemon zest

1 cup sifted confectioners' sugar

6 drops yellow food coloring, optional

Coq Au Vin Du Beaujolais

LES CHEFS DE FRANCE ❋ *EPCOT* ❋ WALT DISNEY WORLD RESORT

SERVES 4

2 pounds bone-in chicken parts
(breasts, wings, drumsticks,
thighs)

½ teaspoon coarse salt

½ teaspoon
freshly ground pepper

1½ ounces salt-pork fat

2 tablespoons butter

6 pearl onions, peeled

¼ pound whole mushrooms,
washed and stems trimmed

2 tablespoons all-purpose flour

1 garlic clove, peeled and
crushed

1 750 ml-size bottle
of Beaujolais wine

2 sprigs fresh thyme
or 2 teaspoons dried

2 sprigs fresh parsley
or 1 tablespoon dried

2 bay leaves

1 to 1½ cups chicken stock

1. Season the chicken with salt and pepper and set aside.

2. Cut the pork fat into ½-inch cubes and place in a small skillet. Cover with cold water and bring to a simmer over medium heat, then reduce heat and simmer for 5 minutes. Drain and pat the cubes dry with paper towels.

3. Preheat oven to 350°F.

4. In a large ovenproof pan, heat butter, pork fat, and pearl onions over medium-high heat on the stove top. When onions are golden brown, remove them and the pork fat with a slotted spoon; set aside.

5. In the same butter, cook the mushrooms over high heat until lightly browned. Remove with a slotted spoon and set aside with the onions.

6. Sauté the chicken in the same pan, over high heat, about 2 minutes on each side, until brown. Sprinkle the chicken with flour and place uncovered in the oven for 5 minutes.

7. Remove chicken from oven and reduce heat to 250°F. Add the garlic to the chicken and stir 1 minute. Return to the stove top, add wine, and bring to a boil, stirring constantly. Add herbs, onions, pork fat,

and mushrooms. Add stock if necessary to cover the meat. Cover the pan and bake in oven for 1½ hours.

8. Remove from oven, place chicken in a serving dish, and strain sauce to remove vegetables. Discard fresh herbs; set aside. Taste sauce, adding salt and pepper to taste. Serve the chicken with the sauce and vegetables poured over it.

9. Serve with hot cooked noodles.

WHAT TO DRINK: Go with George Dubeouf Beaujolais-Villages, matching the wine to the wine in the sauce.

FANCY & FESTIVE

ENTERTAINING IS ONE OF life's great pleasures, so when the occasion calls for fancy, take a little time and create your own culinary masterpiece. Start with the best and freshest ingredients, roll up your sleeves, and chop, simmer, and stir. An elegant dinner party might begin with Napa Rose's sublime Portobello Cappuccino Bisque, or an inspired idea like a crisp stack of Fried Green Tomatoes with Crab and Asiago Cheese from Narcoossee's. Wow your guests with a main course of Rosemary-Grilled Lamb Chops, or Spicy Seared Swordfish with Tomato-Garlic Relish. A perfectly paired wine makes any meal a celebration.

Halibut with Fregole, Chorizo, and Littleneck Clams

FLYING FISH CAFE ✣ *DISNEY'S BOARDWALK RESORT* ✣ WALT DISNEY WORLD RESORT

SERVES 4

5 ounces Spanish chorizo sausage, ¼-inch dice

¼ cup plus 2 tablespoons olive oil, divided

1 small fennel bulb, ¼-inch dice

½ teaspoon dried fennel seeds

3 garlic cloves, chopped

4 shallots, finely diced

3 sprigs fresh thyme, chopped

1 pinch dried chili peppers

1 teaspoon smoked Spanish paprika

1 cup pinot grigio

4 cups chicken stock

Coarse salt and white pepper, to taste

1 cup pearl pasta (fregole)

20 littleneck clams

3 tomatoes, seeds removed, quartered and diced

4 6-ounce halibut fillets

1 tablespoon chopped flat-leaf parsley

1. Preheat oven to 350°F.

2. In a medium stainless steel pot, sauté chorizo in ¼ cup olive oil. Add fennel, fennel seeds, garlic, shallots, thyme, chili peppers, and paprika.

3. Add wine and stir to loosen any brown bits in the bottom of the pan. Simmer until reduced by half.

4. Add chicken stock and season to taste.

5. Add pearl pasta and simmer over medium heat until pasta is al dente.

6. Add clams and tomatoes, cover, and reduce heat to a low simmer.

7. Season halibut with salt and white pepper.

8. Heat a sauté pan and sear the fish in 2 tablespoons olive oil over medium-high heat, about 4 minutes each side. Transfer to oven for 6 to 8 minutes.

9. Check to see if clams have opened. Add fresh parsley and test seasoning.

10. To serve, place 5 clams, broth, and pasta into individual bowls, with halibut on top. Drizzle with extra-virgin olive oil.

COOKS' NOTES: A handful of micro greens on top gives the dish extra color.

WHAT TO DRINK: Elegant, full-bodied Fuedi di San Gregorio, Fiano di Avelino, Campania, a beautifully balanced spicy white.

Fried Green Tomatoes
with Crab & Asiago Cheese

NARCOOSSEE'S ✽ *DISNEY'S GRAND FLORIDIAN RESORT & SPA*

✽ WALT DISNEY WORLD RESORT

SERVES 5

5 small green tomatoes

1¼ cups all-purpose flour

5 large eggs, beaten

2½ cups panko bread crumbs

½ cup olive oil

Coarse salt and freshly
ground pepper, to taste

1 cup lump crabmeat

1¼ cups grated Asiago cheese

15 basil leaves, thinly sliced

25 tarragon leaves, thinly sliced

½ cup thinly sliced
red bell pepper

½ cup thinly sliced red onion

1 tablespoon
extra-virgin olive oil

1 tablespoon balsamic vinegar

Balsamic Reduction
(*recipe follows*)

1. Peel the tomatoes with a vegetable peeler and slice ½ inch thick.

2. Coat tomato slices in flour, then egg, then panko bread crumbs.

3. Heat the olive oil in a sauté pan. Fry the tomato slices on both sides until golden.

4. Season with salt and pepper.

5. Lay the tomato slices in a baking pan and top with crabmeat and Asiago cheese.

6. Broil 2-3 minutes, or until the cheese is fully melted.

7. Stack the layers of tomatoes on top of each other.

8. Toss the basil, tarragon, peppers, onions, olive oil, and vinegar together. Season with salt and pepper to taste and set aside.

9. Place the tomato stack on a plate. Drizzle balsamic reduction over the tomatoes and top with salad.

Balsamic Reduction

1. In a small saucepan over medium heat, reduce the vinegar by 75 percent.

2.   Stir in honey. Set aside until the sauce is a thick consistency. (Do ahead of time.)

1½ cups balsamic vinegar

5 tablespoons honey

COOKS' NOTES: Panko bread crumbs are used in Japanese cooking—they are coarser than most bread crumbs and create a crunchier crust. If you can't find them in your grocery store, try an Asian market.

WHAT TO DRINK: Flavors of lemon, lime, and herbs in Veramonte Sauvignon Blanc, Chile, are balanced and crisply delivered to match this dish.

Tomato and Fresh Mozzarella Salad

VICTORIA & ALBERT'S ❈ *DISNEY'S GRAND FLORIDIAN RESORT & SPA*
❈ *WALT DISNEY WORLD RESORT*

SERVES 6

6 cups heirloom or any variety of tomatoes, peeled, large tomatoes sliced

3 tablespoons extra-virgin olive oil

Coarse salt and freshly ground pepper, to taste

12 arugula leaves

6 red-tip leaf lettuce leaves

6 pitted Niçoise olives

½ cup fresh mozzarella, cut in 12 pieces

1 cup Herb Vinaigrette (*recipe follows*)

6 teaspoons aged balsamic vinegar

1. In a mixing bowl, gently toss tomatoes with olive oil; season with salt and pepper.

2. Arrange tomatoes on serving plates. In the same bowl, toss the arugula and red-tip leaf lettuce, moistening with leftover olive oil. Arrange on plates with tomatoes.

3. Add 1 olive and 2 slices of mozzarella to each plate. Drizzle with the herb vinaigrette and balsamic vinegar.

2 teaspoons Pommery mustard

1 teaspoon Dijon mustard

¼ cup white balsamic vinegar

1 teaspoon chopped chives or scallion

1 teaspoon chopped basil

1 teaspoon chopped parsley

1 cup canola oil

½ teaspoon honey

Coarse salt and freshly ground black pepper, to taste

Herb Vinaigrette

1. In a blender, mix the first 6 ingredients.

2. Gradually add canola oil until well blended. Add honey, and season to taste with salt and pepper.

COOKS' NOTES: Aged balsamic vinegar, available in specialty markets, gets its dark color and pungent sweetness from aging in barrels over a period of years. Beware of those that list sugar as an ingredient—good balsamic relies on aging and refining to define the flavor and quality.

Onion Tart

SERVES 4

1. Preheat oven to 375°F.

2. Heat olive oil in a large skillet over medium heat. Add the onion and bay leaf and sauté about 10 to 15 minutes until soft and lightly browned. Remove to a plate to cool.

3. In a mixing bowl, beat together eggs, cream, milk, and garlic. Season with salt and white pepper and set aside.

4. On a work surface with a rolling pin, roll out the dough to $1/8$-inch thickness. Cut into circles about 4 inches in diameter. Place in tart pans so that they fit in the bottom and up the sides. Trim off the portion over the top if necessary.

5. Prick the dough with the tines of a fork and bake for 5 minutes.

6. Remove from oven and place a teaspoon of sautéed onions in each tart, spreading evenly.

7. Spoon $1½$ tablespoons of egg mixture on top of onions in each tart, then top each with 2 tablespoons blue cheese.

8. Bake at 400°F for 8 to 10 minutes until edges are golden brown.

9. Remove from tart pans and place on serving plates with a drizzle of walnut dressing. Serve warm or at room temperature.

2 tablespoons olive oil

1 large onion,
halved and thinly sliced

1 bay leaf

2 eggs

2 tablespoons heavy cream

2 tablespoons milk

1 garlic clove, minced

Coarse salt and white pepper,
to taste

1 package
refrigerated pie dough

½ cup crumbled blue cheese

4 3½-inch tart pans
(for individual tarts)

Walnut Dressing (*recipe follows*)

Walnut Dressing

FOR 4 TARTS

1. Mix sherry, mustard, walnuts, shallot, salt, and pepper in a blender.

2. Gradually add in the oil until the dressing has a creamy consistency.

WHAT TO DRINK: Sip Sparr Select Pinot Gris, Alsace, a full-bodied, dry wine with ripe apple flavors.

½ cup sherry vinegar

½ teaspoon Dijon mustard

1 tablespoon chopped walnuts

1 small shallot, minced

Coarse salt and freshly cracked
black pepper, to taste

1 cup olive oil

Shrimp Scampi with Orange Harissa

NARCOOSSEE'S ❊ DISNEY'S GRAND FLORIDIAN RESORT & SPA
❊ WALT DISNEY WORLD RESORT

SERVES 4 AS AN APPETIZER OR 2 AS AN ENTREE

2 tablespoons butter

2 tablespoons Harissa
(*recipe follows*)

12 large shrimp, peeled and
deveined, tail on or off

Cilantro, for garnish

1. Melt butter in a skillet or sauté pan over high heat.
   Stir in harissa, then add shrimp and sauté about 3 to
   5 minutes until shrimp are pink, firm, and slightly
   opaque.

2. To serve, garnish with cilantro. Delicious with rice,
   couscous, or bulgur wheat.

Harissa

2 roasted red peppers,
skin removed

2 garlic cloves

½ teaspoon salt

1 teaspoon ground cumin

½ teaspoon ground coriander

¼ cup olive oil

3 tablespoons orange juice

½ teaspoon orange zest

¼ teaspoon red pepper flakes,
optional

Combine all ingredients in food processor or blender to
make a paste. Refrigerate until ready to use.

COOKS' NOTES: You can buy roasted red peppers or make
your own. To roast at home, cut whole peppers in halves
or quarters; remove seeds and membranes. Place on a
foil-lined roasting pan. Broil skin-side up until skins are
blackened. Transfer to a bowl, cover with plastic wrap, and
let peppers steam and cool for 15 to 20 minutes. Peel and
discard the skins.

WHAT TO DRINK: Bright and zesty grapefruit flavors
combined with hints of gooseberry in Kim Crawford
Sauvignon Blanc, New Zealand, pair nicely.

Puget Sound Mussels with Pernod and Grilled Sourdough

ARTIST POINT ❊ *DISNEY'S WILDERNESS LODGE* ❊ WALT DISNEY WORLD RESORT

SERVES 1 AS AN ENTRÉE OR 2 AS AN APPETIZER

1 tablespoon olive oil

1/4 cup fresh chopped parsley

1/2 tablespoon anchovy paste

1 small white onion, diced, and cooked until soft

1 pound Puget Sound mussels washed and debearded

1/4 cup Pernod

1/3 cup white wine

1/4 cup (1/2 stick) unsalted butter

2 tablespoons chopped fennel tops

Toasted sourdough bread

1. Heat a large saucepan (with a lid) over medium heat. When the pan is hot, pour in the olive oil and heat for a few seconds.
2. Add the parsley, anchovy paste, and cooked onions; sauté quickly for 10 seconds to flavor the oil.
3. Add the mussels; stir to coat lightly.
4. Remove from heat and add Pernod. (Pernod is flammable, so use caution, especially with gas stoves.)
5. Return to heat and simmer for 15 seconds. Add the wine and immediately cover.
6. Check after 1 or 2 minutes; as soon as the mussels start to open, remove the lid and continue cooking until the liquid is reduced by half.
7. Lower the heat and add butter. Swirl the pan to mix, then finish by sprinkling chopped fennel over the top.
8. Pour into a bowl and serve with toasted sourdough bread.

WHAT TO DRINK: Try this dish with Moët & Chandon White Star Extra Dry Champagne.

Rosemary Grilled Lamb Chops with White Beans and Marinated Artichokes

NAPA ROSE RESTAURANT ✤ *DISNEY'S GRAND CALIFORNIAN HOTEL & SPA* ✤ DISNEYLAND RESORT

16-20 lamb chops, 1 inch thick

3 tablespoons
finely chopped fresh rosemary

2 tablespoons minced garlic

½ cup extra-virgin olive oil

1 teaspoon dried red chili peppers

2 tablespoons coarse salt

SERVES 8 TO 10

1. Season lamb with rosemary, garlic, olive oil, red chili, and salt; marinate for at least 45 minutes.

2. Grill over medium hot coals for 4-5 minutes each side (for medium rare to medium).

COOKS' NOTES: Lamb porterhouse is a good choice as they are usually meatier than other lamb chops.

White Beans and Marinated Artichokes

¼ cup minced garlic

1 cup finely chopped red onions

1 cup finely chopped fennel

2 tablespoons olive oil

4 cups high-quality cooked
cannellini beans, drained

1 cup marinated baby artichokes

1 cup diced roma tomatoes

1 cup corn

¾ cup chicken stock

1 tablespoon coarse salt

1 tablespoon dried red chili peppers

1 tablespoon lemon zest

2 cups store-bought
white balsamic vinaigrette

¼ cup chopped fresh basil

¼ cup chopped parsley

2 cups fresh baby spinach

1. In a large saucepan over medium heat, sauté garlic, onions, and fennel in olive oil about 7-8 minutes, until vegetables are tender.

2. Add beans, marinated artichokes, tomatoes, corn, and chicken stock; simmer 2 minutes.

3. Add salt, red chili, lemon zest, and white balsamic vinaigrette; simmer 2 more minutes.

4. Add basil, parsley, and spinach. Simmer just until spinach begins to wilt.

5. Serve in a large bowl, family style, or under the lamb chops.

WHAT TO DRINK: Canoe Ridge, Merlot, Columbia Valley, Washington, has a core of pure black cherry and blackberry, and rich full body that stands up to the grilled rosemary flavors.

Grilled Rib-eye of Beef Smothered with Coastal Mushrooms and Blue Cheese "Snow"

Napa Rose Restaurant ❊ *Disney's Grand Californian Hotel & Spa* ❊ Disneyland Resort

Serves 6

Rib-eye steaks (*recipe follows*)

Coarse salt

Cabernet Reduction and Coastal Mushroom Sauce (*recipe follows*)

Panko Crusted Blue Cheese Fries (*recipe follows*)

1 small wedge frozen blue cheese

Watercress for garnish

1. Grill steaks to desired degree of doneness.
2. In a deep pan, heat oil to 375ºF and fry Panko Crusted Blue Cheese Fries until crisp and golden brown. Season with coarse salt.
3. Smother steaks with Cabernet Reduction and Coastal Mushroom Sauce; garnish each plate with two Panko Crusted Blue Cheese Fries.
4. Using a microplane grater, grate frozen blue cheese over the mushroom-smothered steak so that it resembles "snow." Garnish with watercress.

Rib-eye Steaks

½ cup chopped garlic

¼ cup chopped fresh rosemary

1 cup olive oil

1 teaspoon coarse salt

1 teaspoon freshly ground pepper

6 8- to 12-ounce rib-eye steaks

Mix first five ingredients and use to marinate steaks for at least 30 minutes, or refrigerate overnight.

Cabernet Reduction and Coastal Mushroom Sauce

2 tablespoons olive oil

½ cup sliced carrots

⅓ cup sliced onions

⅓ cup sliced celery

1 cup Cabernet wine

4 cups veal stock

⅓ cup white button mushrooms, sliced

2 sprigs fresh thyme

2 sprigs flat-leaf parsley

1 bay leaf

5 black peppercorns

Coarse salt and freshly ground pepper

1. Heat a medium saucepan over medium-high heat, then add olive oil. Stir in carrots, onions, and celery and cook for about 8 to 10 minutes, until vegetables begin to caramelize.

2. Add the Cabernet and deglaze the pan. Reduce liquid by one-half.

3. Add veal stock, white button mushrooms, thyme, parsley, bay leaf, and black peppercorns, and simmer for about 45 minutes, or until the sauce has reduced to desired consistency. Finish by straining through a fine-mesh sieve.

4. Season to taste with salt and pepper. Set aside, keeping warm.

Coastal Mushrooms

1 tablespoon unsalted butter

½ cup portobello mushrooms, washed, stems and gills removed, cut in thin slices

½ cup cremini mushrooms, washed and cut in half

½ cup oyster mushrooms, washed and cut in half

½ cup chanterelle mushrooms, washed and cut in half

¼ cup sliced onion

Coarse salt and freshly ground pepper

1. Melt butter in a medium sauté pan over medium heat. Sauté mushrooms and onion for about 5 minutes, or until tender with slightly toasted edges and liquid is evaporated.

2. Season to taste with salt and pepper. Add to Cabernet reduction.

Panko Crusted Blue Cheese Fries

1. Preheat oven to 425°F.

2. Wrap Yukon Gold potatoes in foil and bake for 45 minutes to 1 hour, or until soft to the touch. While the potatoes are still hot, on a floured working surface, "rice" the potatoes with a food mill.

3. Make a nest in the center of the potatoes and add egg yolks, blue cheese, Parmesan cheese, chives, salt, and pepper. Mix thoroughly.

4. Gently add 1½ cups of the flour, slightly kneading just enough to bring the dough together. The texture should be like soft Play-Doh.

5. Cut dough into long strips and gently roll in the remaining ½ cup flour. When dough is an even log shape, cut into pieces the size of your index finger. Place on parchment paper on a floured baking sheet; wrap and freeze for 12 hours or longer.

6. Dip the frozen strips into egg and then panko bread crumbs. Refreeze.

WHAT TO DRINK: Silverado Vineyards, Cabernet Sauvignon, Napa Valley, brimming with aromas of cassis and blackberries.

3 large Yukon Gold potatoes

3 egg yolks

¼ cup crumbled blue cheese

¼ cup grated Parmesan cheese

2 tablespoons chopped chives

Coarse salt and coarsely ground pepper, to taste

2 cups flour, divided

2 eggs, beaten

2 cups panko bread crumbs

Trout Meunière with Pan-Roasted Pecan Sauce

BLUE BAYOU RESTAURANT ✳ *DISNEYLAND PARK* ✳ DISNEYLAND RESORT

SERVES 4

1. In a shallow dish, mix flour, salt, white pepper, and cayenne. Set aside.

2. In a large skillet or sauté pan over medium-high heat, add clarified butter, reserving 1 tablespoon.

3. Dredge trout in milk, then in flour mixture, and add to hot skillet. Cook over medium-high heat 2 minutes on each side, or until golden brown. Remove to a serving platter, and keep warm.

4. Wipe out the pan and return to heat, adding last tablespoon of clarified butter. Add shallots and sauté about 10 seconds. Add chopped pecans and sauté 1 minute. Add a pinch of flour, then whisk in wine and lemon juice, whisking about 30 seconds until smooth and shiny.

5. Remove from heat and add unsalted butter and parsley, then season to taste with salt and pepper. Spoon sauce over fish and serve immediately.

COOKS' NOTES: To make clarified butter, slowly melt unsalted butter until the milk solids sink to the bottom of the pan. Do not stir. The golden liquid on top is clarified butter. (Skim off any foam.)

WHAT TO DRINK: Baileyana Vineyards, Chardonnay Grand Firepeak Cuvee, Edna Valley, with ripe tropical flavors of fresh pineapple, citrus, and pear, and a slight creaminess to complement the fish.

1 cup flour

¾ tablespoon salt

¼ teaspoon white pepper

Pinch cayenne pepper

¼ cup clarified butter, divided

4 8-ounce trout fillets

1 cup milk

1 tablespoon minced shallots

¾ cup chopped pecans

Pinch of flour

¼ cup white wine

Juice of 1 lemon

3 tablespoons unsalted butter

1 tablespoon chopped parsley

Coarse salt and freshly ground pepper

Portobello Cappuccino Bisque with Brandied Thyme Froth

NAPA ROSE RESTAURANT ❊ *DISNEY'S GRAND CALIFORNIAN HOTEL & SPA*
❊ DISNEYLAND RESORT

SERVES 6

Portobello Cappuccino Bisque
(*recipe follows*)

Brandied Thyme Froth
(*recipe follows*)

FINISHES:

1 cup julienned portobello
mushrooms (stems and gills
removed)

½ cup thinly sliced scallions
(both green and white parts)

Olive oil for sautéing

2 tablespoons
chopped fresh thyme

1 tablespoon
chopped fresh sage

1 teaspoon fresh lemon juice

Coarse salt and freshly cracked
pepper, to taste

1. In separate pans, sauté portobello mushrooms and scallions in olive oil. Set aside.

2. To hot bisque, add sautéed mushrooms, scallions, thyme, sage, and lemon juice. Season to taste with salt and pepper.

3. Warm 6 coffee cups, then spoon equal amounts of portobello mushrooms into each cup. Add bisque and top with brandied thyme froth.

Portobello Cappuccino Bisque

1. Sauté shallots in butter until translucent.

2. Add mushrooms and sauté 7–10 minutes until released juices have evaporated.

3. Add sherry and reduce by half; add demi-glace, cream, and herbs. Simmer for 25 minutes.

4. Strain and serve with Brandied Thyme Froth and garnishes, or reheat to serve.

COOKS' NOTES: The "cappuccino" can be prepared the day before.

½ cup sliced shallots

1 tablespoon butter

1 cup sliced portobello mushrooms, gills removed

2 cups sliced white mushrooms

½ cup medium-dry sherry

1 cup veal demi-glace (from gourmet grocery)

1 quart heavy cream

1 small bunch thyme stems

2 bay leaves

Brandied Thyme Froth

Place all ingredients in mixing bowl and whip until soft peaks form.

WHAT TO DRINK: Ruby-rose Goldeneye Vineyards, Pinot Noir, Anderson Valley, Mendocino, a perfect match with mushrooms.

1 cup cold heavy whipping cream

2 tablespoons chopped fresh thyme

½ teaspoon salt

¼ teaspoon black pepper

2 tablespoons brandy or cognac

Spicy Seared Swordfish with Tomato-Garlic Relish

STORYTELLERS CAFE ❋ DISNEY'S GRAND CALIFORNIAN HOTEL & SPA ❋ DISNEYLAND RESORT

SERVES 4

4 swordfish fillets, 6 ounces each

Olive oil, as needed

4 teaspoons Cajun spice

Tomato-Garlic Relish (*recipe follows*)

1. Lightly coat swordfish with olive oil, rub with Cajun spice, and sear both sides in a hot sauté pan, 2 to 3 minutes on each side, or to desired doneness.

2. Top with relish and serve immediately.

Tomato-Garlic Relish

5 roma tomatoes

¼ cup extra-virgin olive oil

1 garlic clove, minced

½ medium sweet white onion, diced large

¼ cup olive oil

1 green pepper, seeded and diced

¼ cup dry white wine

1 teaspoon balsamic vinegar

1 teaspoon Cajun spice, or to taste

1. Preheat oven to 375°F.

2. Drizzle tomatoes with olive oil and bake 30 minutes, until tender but not too soft.

3. Let tomatoes cool, then peel skins and squeeze out seeds. Chop in large chunks and set aside.

4. In a medium saucepan over high heat, sauté garlic and onions in olive oil. Add the green pepper and sauté until tender.

5. Stir in wine and balsamic vinegar, loosening browned bits on the bottom of the pan. Add tomatoes and season with Cajun spice.

COOKS' NOTES: The tomato-garlic relish can be made ahead of time, then warmed just before serving.

WHAT TO DRINK: Robert Weil, Riesling Spatlese, Kedrich Grafenberg, Rheingau, Germany—a sweet Riesling that pairs well with this spicy dish. The sugar of the wine cools down the Cajun heat, and the spiciness pulls the sweetness away from the wine, leaving an incredible fruit flavor.

THE GORGEOUS COLORS of a garden on a plate: Jiko's Cucumber, Tomato, and Red Onion Salad; Field Greens with Grilled Salmon from Storytellers Cafe; apple, dried berries, and baby greens from Artist's Palette. These stylish, mouthwatering recipes from the Disney chefs show off a lighter, more healthful

FRESH & HEALTHFUL

style of eating. And talk about easy—the flavorful dishes can either be made ahead or tossed together in less than 30 minutes. More time for an after-dinner walk.

Papaya, Avocado, and Grapefruit Salad

BOMA—FLAVORS OF AFRICA ✳ *DISNEY'S ANIMAL KINGDOM LODGE*
✳ *WALT DISNEY WORLD RESORT*

SERVES 4 TO 6

1 papaya, at least 10 ounces

1 ripe but firm avocado

1 grapefruit

10 mint leaves, julienned

½ cup plain yogurt

2 tablespoons grapefruit juice

1 tablespoon honey

1. Peel the papaya, halve, and scoop out the seeds. Dice into 1-inch cubes.

2. Slice avocado lengthwise all the way around to the pit. Gently twist the sides in opposite directions to separate halves. Remove the pit. Slip a large spoon in between the skin and the meat and scoop out the flesh. Cut into 1-inch cubes.

3. In a large bowl, peel and section the grapefruit, letting the pieces fall into a bowl. (Reserve juice for the dressing.)

4. Add the papaya, avocado, and mint leaves; set aside.

5. In a small bowl, stir together yogurt, grapefruit juice, and honey.

6. Pour the dressing over the fruit and toss gently.

WHAT TO DRINK: With tropical fruit character, Hamilton Russell Chardonnay, Walker Bay, complements this healthy salad.

Lentil and Kale Stew

SERVES 8

1 pound petite French lentils

2 teaspoons sea salt, divided

½ cup olive oil

1 bay leaf

1 cup chopped onion

2 stalks celery,
washed and chopped

2 carrots, peeled and chopped

2 garlic cloves, mashed

6 ounces kale,
washed and thinly sliced

5 tomatoes,
peeled and chopped

3 14.5-ounce cans
fat-free chicken broth

1 cup fresh parsley, chopped

1 teaspoon freshly ground
black pepper

freshly grated Parmesan
cheese

extra-virgin olive oil

1. Rinse lentils and pick over for small rocks or pieces of hull.

2. Place lentils in a soup pot and cover with water; add 1 teaspoon of the sea salt. Bring to a boil and cook for 5 minutes. Drain, rinse, and set aside.

3. In the same pot, heat the olive oil with the bay leaf, onions, celery, carrots, and garlic. Stir in kale; simmer 5 minutes. Add tomatoes.

4. Add cooked lentils, chicken stock, and remaining sea salt. Bring to a boil; lower the heat and simmer, partially covered, for 15 minutes.

5. Add parsley and black pepper. Season to taste. Top with grated Parmesan cheese and olive oil, if desired.

COOKS' NOTES: If you can't find kale, use chard or spinach. The tiny French (green) lentils, available at specialty stores and in bulk at many natural food stores, have a more delicate flavor than brown lentils, and keep their shape and color. This soup tastes better a day after it's made.

WHAT TO DRINK: Pour Paul Cluver Pinot Noir, Elgin, with a touch of earthiness and a smoky cherry profile.

Cucumber, Tomato, and Red Onion Salad

JIKO—THE COOKING PLACE ❋ *DISNEY'S ANIMAL KINGDOM LODGE* ❋ WALT DISNEY WORLD RESORT

SERVES 4

1 English cucumber

½ teaspoon coarse salt

½ red onion, very thinly sliced

2 tomatoes, cubed

Vanilla Dressing (*recipe follows*)

Coarse salt and freshly ground black pepper, to taste

Melon Vinaigrette (*recipe follows*)

¼ pound arugula

1. Cut cucumber in half, seed, slice fine, and place in a stainless steel bowl.
2. Add salt, mix well, and let sit for 30 minutes at room temperature.
3. Drain water from cucumber and mix with onions and tomatoes.
4. Add ¼ cup of vanilla dressing (reserve the rest) and season with salt and pepper to taste.
5. In the center of a large plate, mound the tomato, cucumber, and red onions and drizzle 2 tablespoons of melon vinaigrette around them.
6. Top with the arugula tossed with 2 tablespoons of vanilla dressing.

Vanilla Dressing

½ cup white balsamic vinegar (you may substitute malt or cider vinegar, but do not use brown balsamic)

½ tablespoon vanilla extract

¼ cup extra-virgin olive oil

Coarse salt and freshly ground black pepper, to taste

Whisk all the ingredients together, adjust seasoning to taste, and set aside.

(continued)

Melon Vinaigrette

¼ cup cantaloupe juice

6 tablespoons watermelon juice

Pinch each of coarse salt and freshly ground black pepper

¼ cup fresh lemon juice

½ cup extra-virgin olive oil

¼ cup cottage cheese

½ tablespoon finely sliced basil leaves

1. Juice the cantaloupe and watermelon (cut into small pieces and squeeze by hand or use an old-fashioned glass or metal orange juicer) and measure amounts needed.

2. Mix in salt and pepper, then lemon juice.

3. Whisk in olive oil and adjust seasoning. Set aside.

4. When ready to serve, mix in cottage cheese and basil.

COOKS' NOTES: Both dressings can be made the day before and kept refrigerated. Never refrigerate tomatoes—they are more flavorful at room temperature.

WHAT TO DRINK: Pair with Mulderbosch Sauvignon Blanc, Stellenbosch. The flavors of ripe pink grapefruit and guava extend the wine's crispness through this refreshing salad.

Fattoush Salad

GASPARILLA GRILL & GAMES ✽ DISNEY'S GRAND FLORIDIAN RESORT & SPA ✽ WALT DISNEY WORLD RESORT

SERVES 6

1. In a large serving bowl, mix together first 7 ingredients.

2. In a small bowl, whisk together garlic, salt, pepper, lemon juice, and olive oil. Stir into salad.

COOKS' NOTES: Use only the crisp hearts of romaine lettuce, saving the outer leaves for another salad. A traditional Fattoush Salad usually includes cheese and chunks of bread, so you can also add feta cheese (2/3 cup) and toss in bite-size pieces of toasted pita bread or chewy foccacia.

3 hearts of romaine lettuce, chopped

1 cup thinly sliced radishes

½ cup diced red onion

1 cucumber, peeled and diced

2 cups diced tomatoes

½ bunch parsley, chopped

¼ cup finely chopped mint

6 garlic cloves, minced

2 teaspoons coarse salt

2 teaspoons freshly ground black pepper

¼ cup fresh lemon juice

5 tablespoons extra-virgin olive oil

Field Greens Salad with Grilled Salmon

STORYTELLERS CAFE ❄ DISNEY'S GRAND CALIFORNIAN HOTEL & SPA ❄ DISNEYLAND RESORT

SERVES 4

1 pound fresh green beans

1 pound salmon,
cut into 4 equal pieces

Coarse salt and freshly ground
black pepper

1 tablespoon olive oil

4 cups mixed spring greens

1 cup Honey Balsamic
Vinaigrette (*recipe follows*)

⅓ cup orange zest

⅓ cup chopped chives

1. Plunge green beans into boiling water for 5 minutes, until partly cooked. Drain and refresh in iced water. Set aside.

2. Season salmon with salt and pepper, and brush with olive oil. Grill over medium-high heat about 5 minutes, just until done.

3. Divide greens and green beans equally on 4 plates. Place salmon on top of salad, drizzle with Honey Balsamic Vinaigrette. Garnish with orange zest and chives.

Honey Balsamic Vinaigrette

¼ cup honey

½ cup balsamic vinegar

1 cup olive oil

2 cloves of garlic, chopped

2 shallots, minced

Coarse salt and freshly ground
black pepper, to taste

Whisk ingredients together.

WHAT TO DRINK: Crocker & Starr Sauvignon Blanc, Napa Valley, has a citrusy, almost tangerine, finish that pairs well with the salmon.

Roasted Vegetable Cuban Sandwich

SUNSHINE SEASONS ✻ THE LAND, EPCOT ✻ WALT DISNEY WORLD RESORT

SERVES 4

3 portobello mushrooms

Olive oil as needed, for grilling

8 ounces fresh eggplant, unpeeled, cut in half lengthwise

8 ounces yellow squash, cut in half lengthwise

8 ounces zucchini, cut in half lengthwise

1 red pepper, sliced

Coarse salt and freshly ground black pepper, to taste

1 teaspoon olive oil

1 24-inch Cuban bread roll

¼ cup store-bought hummus

1 tablespoon yellow mustard

4 slices Swiss cheese

¼ cup or more sliced sour pickles

1. Preheat oven to 400°F.

2. Carefully remove the stems from portobello mushrooms and wipe the caps. Brush olive oil on both sides, then grill 8 to 10 minutes on each side until mushrooms begin to brown and are soft to the touch. Refrigerate.

3. Season eggplant, squash, zucchini, and red pepper with salt and pepper; drizzle with olive oil and roast for 15 minutes. Refrigerate.

4. Slice chilled vegetables into ¼-inch planks. Slice chilled portobello into ¼-inch rounds.

5. Slice Cuban bread lengthwise. Spread top with hummus. Spread bottom with mustard. Arrange vegetables evenly on the bread and top with Swiss cheese and pickles.

6. Brush griddle or skillet with oil and grill for 2 to 3 minutes on each side, or until bread is crusty and cheese is melted. Cut into 4 servings.

WHAT TO DRINK: Guenoc Sauvignon Blanc, California, with zesty lime with herbal grass notes, works well with the fresh veggies.

Saratoga Springs House Salad

THE ARTIST'S PALETTE ❋ *DISNEY'S SARATOGA SPRINGS RESORT & SPA*
❋ WALT DISNEY WORLD RESORT

4 cups gourmet salad mix

4 tablespoons dried cranberries

2 tablespoons dried blueberries

½ unpeeled red apple, diced

2 tablespoons chopped walnuts

½ cup Poppy Seed Dressing (*recipe follows*)

SERVES 4

1. Combine all ingredients in a large bowl; toss gently. Serve with Poppy Seed Dressing.

Poppy Seed Dressing

1. Combine first five ingredients in blender or food processor and process for 20 seconds.

2. With blender on high, gradually add oil in a slow, steady stream. Stir in poppy seeds.

¼ cup sugar

¼ cup fresh lemon juice

1 teaspoon diced onion

½ teaspoon Dijon mustard

¼ teaspoon coarse salt

6 tablespoons canola oil

1½ teaspoons poppy seeds

Edamame Salad

SERVES 4 TO 6

1. Cook fresh or frozen beans in boiling, salted water for 3 minutes, then chill.

2. In a small mixing bowl, combine vinegar, sesame oil, salt, napa cabbage, and bok choy. Let sit at room temperature for 20 minutes. (Cabbage will wilt slightly.)

3. Mix in carrots, then refrigerate for 1 hour.

4. To serve, top with sesame seeds and daikon radish.

COOKS' NOTES: Edamame can be found in most supermarkets in the frozen-foods section. Daikon radishes are often in the supermarket, or you can find them at the local Asian grocery (red radishes are not a good substitute).

4 cups edamame (young soybeans), fresh or frozen

½ cup rice wine vinegar

¼ cup sesame oil

1 teaspoon coarse salt

1 cup chopped napa cabbage

½ cup chopped bok choy

½ cup shredded carrots

1 tablespoon black sesame seeds

¼ cup shredded white daikon radish

MAXIMUM FLAVOR, *minimum effort.*
When you're too busy to cook, these casual
creations are a quick flash in the pan. Make

a one-dish dinner with Cítricos'
peppery Arugula Salad with thin
slices of salty, sweet prosciutto
and crisp Napa Rose Lavosh.

Seafood is a snap, like Spoodles' quick sauté
of Lemon Garlic Shrimp; or fresh mussels with

FAST & CASUAL

a splash of coconut
milk, fresh ginger,

and curry from Kona Cafe. Sophisticated but
undemanding, these meals are ready
in minutes—but taste like special
occasions. Even a favorite
Disney dessert goes together
in seconds in a blender.

Grilled Shrimp and Seared Scallop Pasta

DISNEY MAGIC & DISNEY WONDER ✳ DISNEY CRUISE LINE

SERVES 4

8 ounces linguine

2 cups favorite spaghetti sauce

2 garlic cloves, thinly sliced

5 tablespoons butter, divided

2 cups fresh spinach

Coarse salt and freshly ground white pepper

12 large shrimp, peeled and deveined

12 large scallops

1. Cook linguine according to package directions; drain and mix with spaghetti sauce. Keep warm.

2. In a large skillet, sauté garlic in 2 tablespoons butter until golden; add spinach and cook until wilted. Season with salt and pepper, and set aside.

3. Heat remaining 3 tablespoons butter in a skillet over medium-high heat; add shrimp and scallops, and cook about 3 minutes, or until shrimp turn pink and scallops are white, turning once.

4. Top pasta with cooked spinach, and serve with shrimp and scallops arranged around the pasta.

WHAT TO DRINK: From the Loire, crisp Pascal Jolivet Sancerre Sauvignon Blanc works beautifully with the shellfish.

Lemon Garlic Shrimp

SPOODLES ❋ *DISNEY'S BOARDWALK RESORT* ❋ *WALT DISNEY WORLD RESORT*

SERVES 6

½ cup (1 stick) unsalted butter, divided

3 garlic cloves, finely chopped, divided

36 large shrimp, deveined and butterflied

¼ cup fresh lemon juice

½ teaspoon coarse salt

⅛ teaspoon freshly cracked black pepper

½ bunch parsley, roughly chopped

1. Melt half the butter in a sauté pan. Add half the garlic and sauté until just golden.

2. Add shrimp and toss to coat. Cook about 1–2 minutes on each side until shrimp is almost done—pink, firm, and slightly opaque.

3. Add lemon juice and remaining garlic and butter. Do not boil.

4. Season with salt and pepper; toss in parsley. Delicious as an appetizer, or as a sauce for pasta.

COOKS' NOTES: To butterfly shrimp, split down the center lengthwise, cutting almost but not completely through. Then open the two halves flat to resemble a butterfly shape.

WHAT TO DRINK: The crisp and delicate lemon citrus flavors of Satori Pinot Grigio, delle Venezie are a delightful accompaniment.

Steakhouse Salad

SERVES 4

1. In a large bowl, mix beef tips with pepper, oregano, garlic, salt, vinegar, and ½ cup olive oil. Marinate at least 2 hours.

2. In a small bowl, whisk together dry mustard, sugar, salt, pepper, and vinegar; drizzle in 1 cup of olive oil, continuing to whisk. Set aside.

3. In a skillet over medium-high heat, sauté beef tips in remaining 2 tablespoons of olive oil until desired degree of doneness. Remove from stove and keep warm.

4. In a salad bowl, mix lettuce, tomatoes, onion, and beef. Garnish with goat cheese and chives, and serve with tortillas.

WHAT TO DRINK: You'll enjoy Cantena Malbec, Mendoza, a juicy blackberry-style wine with full-bodied character and soft tannins.

1 pound beef tenderloin tips, diced into ¼-inch cubes

1 teaspoon black pepper

2 teaspoons dried oregano

2 teaspoons minced garlic

2 teaspoons salt

¼ cup vinegar

1½ cups plus 2 tablespoons olive oil, divided

1½ tablespoons dry mustard

1 tablespoon sugar

⅛ teaspoon salt

⅛ teaspoon black pepper

2 tablespoons white balsamic vinegar

4 cups chopped bibb lettuce

½ cup diced tomatoes

¼ cup thinly sliced red onion

½ cup crumbled goat cheese

2 tablespoons chopped chives

4 tortillas, grilled and quartered

Mediterranean Seafood Lime Salad

CÍTRICOS ✳ DISNEY'S GRAND FLORIDIAN RESORT & SPA ✳ WALT DISNEY WORLD RESORT

SERVES 6 TO 8 AS AN APPETIZER

1. Combine all ingredients and marinate at least 1 hour before serving.

COOKS' NOTES: This salad goes together easily with precooked shrimp and mussels from the market. If not, allow plenty of time to steam and chill the mussels and shrimp.

WHAT TO DRINK: From the northwest province in Spain comes Nora Albarino, Rias Biaxus, a refreshing, lime-accented, dry white with floral notes of white peach—a natural complement to this salad.

½ cup fresh lime juice

½ cup olive oil

1 large tomato, seeded and diced, about 1½ cups

⅓ cup minced red onion

1 cup peeled, diced cucumber

1½ cups cooked, diced shrimp

¾ cup crabmeat

2 dozen mussels, cooked and removed from shells

½ cup chopped fresh basil

⅓ cup chopped fresh mint

1 teaspoon red chili flakes

Coarse salt and white pepper, to taste

Mussels in Green Thai Broth

KONA CAFE ✻ *DISNEY'S POLYNESIAN RESORT* ✻ WALT DISNEY WORLD RESORT

SERVES 4

¼ cup canola oil

2 cups yellow onions, cut into very thin strips

2 cups green tomatoes, diced ¼-inch pieces

2 tablespoons minced fresh ginger

2 tablespoons minced fresh garlic

4 teaspoons Thai green curry paste (available in Asian specialty markets)

½ cup (1 stick) salted butter, softened

2 cups coconut milk

4 pounds live mussels

Coarse salt and freshly ground pepper, to taste

4 limes, thinly sliced (about 24 slices)

1 cup chopped cilantro

4 slices day-old Italian bread

1. Place wok or large saucepan, uncovered, over high heat until hot. Add oil, then onions and tomatoes, and sauté for 1 minute. Add ginger and garlic and stir for 1 to 2 minutes, until the onions are slightly softened.

2. Stir in curry paste, butter, and coconut milk. Add mussels and season with salt and pepper. Add lime slices; cover the pan and steam over medium-high heat for 5 minutes, or until the mussels open.

3. Add cilantro and pour into a large serving bowl. Garnish with bread slices (great for soaking up the broth).

COOKS' NOTES: Mussels are best when cooked as soon as possible. Wash with a stiff kitchen brush under cool running water and remove the beard. Discard any with broken shells. And never eat a mussel whose shell is not open after cooking.

WHAT TO DRINK: Open a bottle of Wynn's Coonawarra Riesling, Australia, a refreshing peach-scented white with a crisp and dry mineral expression that works well with the spicy broth.

Arugula Salad with Prosciutto Ham

Cítricos ❋ *Disney's Grand Floridian Resort & Spa* ❋ *Walt Disney World Resort*

SERVES 4

Divide arugula among 4 serving plates. Drizzle with vinaigrette. Drape 2 slices of prosciutto over the greens, then garnish with olives, shaved Parmesan cheese, and croutons.

4 cups arugula

4 tablespoons Vinaigrette Dressing (*recipe follows*)

8 slices
thinly sliced prosciutto

Olives, shaved Parmesan cheese, and croutons
for garnish

Vinaigrette Dressing

In a small bowl, whisk together mustard, lemon juice, and sherry vinegar. Gradually whisk in olive oil. Taste and season with salt and pepper.

WHAT TO DRINK: Crisp, white Gini Soave Classico, Veneto, from the rolling hills of Italy, matches with the bitterness of the greens and the slightly salty flavor from the prosciutto.

2 teaspoons Dijon mustard

2 tablespoons fresh lemon juice

2 tablespoons sherry vinegar

⅔ cup olive oil

Coarse salt and freshly ground pepper, to taste

Kona Salad

SERVES 8

3 unpeeled Asian pears,
cored and thinly sliced

9 cups (or 1-pound bag) spring
mix or gourmet lettuce mix

1 cup crumbled blue cheese

¼ cup thinly sliced red onion

¾ cup smoked almonds,
chopped in large pieces

6 tablespoons
fresh-squeezed orange juice

2 tablespoons rice vinegar

1 teaspoon granulated sugar

½ cup canola oil

¼ teaspoon coarse salt

⅛ teaspoon freshly ground
black pepper

1.   In a large bowl, gently toss pears, salad mix, blue cheese, onion, and almonds.

2.   In a separate bowl, mix orange juice, rice vinegar, and sugar. Whisk in canola oil, salt, and pepper.

3.   Pour over salad and gently toss; serve immediately.

COOKS' NOTES: If Asian pears are not available, you can substitute fresh peaches, strawberries, or other berries—whatever is in season.

WHAT TO DRINK: This refreshing salad requires a light, crisp wine like Dr. Thanisch Graccher Himmelreich Riesling Spätlese, Mosel-Saar Ruwer—a great match.

Napa Rose Lavosh

NAPA ROSE RESTAURANT ❇ *DISNEY'S GRAND CALIFORNIAN HOTEL & SPA* ❇ DISNEYLAND RESORT

SERVES A CROWD

1 cup extra-virgin olive oil

2 large garlic cloves, smashed

2 teaspoons finely chopped parsley

Coarse salt and freshly ground black pepper

1 package lavosh (this flatbread can be purchased in Indian and other specialty food markets)

1 cup grated Parmigiano-Reggiano cheese

1. In bowl, mix olive oil with garlic and parsley; season with salt and pepper.
2. Brush lavosh with olive-oil mixture and sprinkle with cheese.
3. Bake at 350°F for 8 minutes, or until golden brown and lightly crisp. Serve warm, or cooled, as a cracker, with appetizers.

S'mores

50's Prime Time Cafe ❈ *Disney-MGM Studios* ❈ Walt Disney World Resort

Serves 2

2 graham crackers

2 Hershey's chocolate bars

12 marshmallows

4 tablespoons chocolate syrup

1. Lay graham crackers on plate, side by side. Cover with chocolate bars.

2. Broil for a few seconds to soften chocolate.

3. Put 6 marshmallows on each cracker; broil until browned.

4. Drizzle chocolate syrup over the top.

Peanut Butter 'n Jelly Shake

50's Prime Time Cafe ❈ *Disney-MGM Studios* ❈ Walt Disney World Resort

Makes 1 shake

2 tablespoons peanut butter

2 tablespoons grape jelly

2 cups vanilla ice cream

¼ cup milk

Blend ingredients until smooth and thick.

DELICIEUX. KÖSTLICH. Delicioso.

Delizioso! In a mile-long stroll
around Epcot World Showcase,
you can go around the
globe in a day—deliciously
noshing your way through
11 international cultures. Taste
Bouillabaisse Provençale in France,
Italy's Fettuccine Alfredo, hearty Guinness Stew

INTERNATIONALCUISINE

from the United Kingdom, Morocco's Chicken
Tagine. The international flair extends beyond
Epcot as Disney chefs create dishes from

regions as diverse as South Africa,
Thailand, and the Mediterranean.
With these recipes there's no need for
a passport or suitcase, you've got the
world in your kitchen.

Seared Scallops with Chakalaka and Crisp Mealie Pap

JIKO—THE COOKING PLACE ❊ *DISNEY'S ANIMAL KINGDOM LODGE* ❊ WALT DISNEY WORLD RESORT

SERVES 6

Mealie Pap (*recipe follows*)

Chakalaka (*recipe follows*)

4 tablespoons butter, divided

30 large fresh scallops

Coarse salt and freshly ground black pepper, to taste

2 tablespoons olive oil

1 bunch cilantro, finely chopped

1. Make Mealie Pap. While Mealie Pap is cooling, make Chakalaka and keep warm.
2. Cut Mealie Pap into 6 slices. Brown in a nonstick pan in 2 tablespoons of butter until golden on both sides. Keep warm.
3. Remove muscle from scallops and dry scallops on a paper towel. Season with salt and pepper.
4. Heat olive oil in a nonstick pan over medium-high heat. Sear scallops about 3 minutes each side, until golden brown. When you turn the scallops to brown the other side, add 2 tablespoons butter.
5. To serve, place scallops and Mealie Pap on warm Chakalaka with Mealie Pap cake on top. Garnish with chopped cilantro and serve immediately.

Crisp Cornmeal or "Mealie Pap"

2 cups water

½ cup white cornmeal

Coarse salt and freshly ground black pepper, to taste

1. Bring water to a boil in a heavy-bottomed stainless steel saucepan. Slowly whisk in the white cornmeal and cook according to package directions. Season with salt and pepper.
2. Pour the "pap" into an 8-inch square buttered pan and refrigerate to cool. (Or put in freezer to shorten cooling time.)

Chakalaka

1. In a heavy-bottomed stainless steel pot, heat the olive oil. Add diced onions and sauté until opaque.

2. Add diced tomatoes and chopped jalapeño; cook for about 2 minutes more.

3. Add sugar, salt, and freshly ground black pepper; mix well. Remove from heat and adjust seasoning to taste. Keep warm until ready to serve.

WHAT TO DRINK: The full-bodied flavors of Fairview Viognier, Paarl, are a nice contrast to the delicate sweetness of this scallop dish.

2 tablespoons olive oil

1 medium Spanish onion, diced large

4 large tomatoes, diced large

1 jalapeño chili, seeded and finely chopped

½ teaspoon sugar

Coarse salt and freshly ground black pepper, to taste

Cape Malay Lamb Curry

SERVES 4 TO 6

2 pounds lamb,
shoulder or leg meat

Coarse salt and freshly ground
pepper, to taste

2 tablespoons vegetable oil

2 large onions, diced

2 green chilies,
seeded and finely sliced

1 teaspoon crushed garlic

1 teaspoon
crushed fresh ginger

1 to 4 tablespoons
Madras curry powder

1 tablespoon flour

3 to 4 large vine-ripened
tomatoes, chopped

3 tablespoons
cream of coconut

1 cup chicken stock

1 tablespoon
fresh chopped cilantro

1. Trim fat from lamb and cut into 1-inch cubes. Season with salt and pepper.

2. Heat oil in a large skillet over medium-high heat. Add lamb and sear until browned, stirring often. Remove lamb.

3. Add onions and cook until lightly browned and tender. Add chilies, garlic, and ginger; cook 2 minutes. Add curry powder and cook 1 minute.

4. Whisk in flour and stir over low heat until flour is cooked and the mixture has thickened slightly. Stir in tomatoes, cream of coconut, and chicken stock; return lamb to the pan. If too thick, stir in more chicken stock.

5. Cover and simmer for 45–50 minutes, or until the lamb is tender. Stir occasionally to avoid burning.

6. Taste and adjust seasonings. To serve, garnish with cilantro and serve with rice pilaf or couscous.

COOKS' NOTES: Curry powder is actually a blend of up to 20 spices, herbs, and seeds. Commercial curry powder comes in two basic styles—standard, and the hotter Madras. Curry powder should be stored no longer than 2 months in an airtight container.

WHAT TO DRINK: The smoky cherry flavors combined with juicy blackberry notes of Cape Indaba Shiraz, South Africa, pair well with the full flavors of this lamb dish.

Crispy Polenta with Mushrooms, Wilted Greens, and Balsamic Vinaigrette

SPOODLES ❋ *DISNEY'S BOARDWALK RESORT* ❋ WALT DISNEY WORLD RESORT

SERVES 4

1. In a large mixing bowl, stir together cooked polenta with 4 tablespoons of butter. Season to taste with salt and pepper.

2. Pour polenta to ½-inch thickness in an 8-inch square pan. Refrigerate for 2 hours.

3. While polenta is cooling, make Balsamic Vinaigrette. Set aside.

4. In a sauté pan, whisk together wine and vegetable stock; cook until reduced by half. Remove from pan and set aside.

5. In the same pan, heat 2 tablespoons of olive oil and sauté the mushrooms.

6. Add the wine and stock reduction to the mushrooms; cook 2 minutes. Season to taste with salt and pepper. Remove from pan and keep warm until ready to serve.

7. In the same pan, melt the remaining 1 tablespoon butter. Add greens and water and cook just until greens are wilted. Keep warm.

8. Remove polenta from refrigerator and cut into 8 squares.

9. In a large skillet, heat the remaining 2 tablespoons olive oil and cook the polenta until crispy, turning once.

10. Place wilted greens on serving plates, top each with 2 squares of warm polenta, then spoon mushrooms over the top. Drizzle with vinaigrette.

(continued)

---

2 cups warm cooked polenta or any cooked cornmeal

5 tablespoons butter, divided

Coarse salt and freshly ground black pepper, to taste

Balsamic Vinaigrette (*recipe follows*)

½ cup red wine

1 cup vegetable stock

4 tablespoons olive oil, divided, more as needed for panfrying polenta

1 cup shiitake mushrooms

1 cup cremini mushrooms

2 cups Swiss chard or large-leaf spinach

2 cups arugula

2 tablespoons water

Balsamic Vinaigrette

1 shallot, minced

3 tablespoons balsamic vinegar

½ teaspoon fresh thyme, basil, or other favorite herb

5 tablespoons olive oil

Coarse salt and freshly ground black pepper, to taste

1. In a food processor or blender, mix together shallots, vinegar, and herbs.

2. Drizzle in olive oil with machine running.

3. Season with salt and pepper, to taste.

COOKS' NOTES: Two cups of white mushrooms can be substituted for cremini and shiitake mushrooms.

WHAT TO DRINK: Fess Parker Chardonnay, Santa Barbara, accents the sweet corn flavors of the polenta and complements the earthiness of the mushrooms.

Honey and Chili-Garlic Snapper with Green Papaya Salad and Thai-style Pesto

CATERING CHEFS ❊ *DISNEY-MGM STUDIOS CATERING* ❊ WALT DISNEY WORLD RESORT

SERVES 4

1½ pounds fresh snapper fillets (skin on, approximately 6 ounces per person)

¼ cup light vegetable oil

Coarse salt and freshly ground black pepper, to taste

½ cup honey

½ cup rice vinegar

¼ cup chili-garlic sauce

Green Papaya Salad (*recipe follows*)

Thai Pesto (*recipe follows*)

Chili oil, optional

OPTIONAL GARNISHES: chopped peanuts, chopped cilantro, and lime wedges

1. Toss the snapper with oil, salt, and pepper.
2. To make a glaze, combine honey, vinegar, and chili-garlic sauce in a small saucepan and reduce to about ¾ cup.
3. In a heavy skillet, pan sear the snapper over medium-high heat, skin side down; turn once and brush often with the glaze. Cook 3 to 4 minutes each side, turning once and brushing with glaze.
4. Serve on top of papaya salad with a dollop of Thai pesto, and a drizzle of chili oil, if desired.
5. Garnish with chopped peanuts, cilantro, and limes, if desired.

(Continued)

Green Papaya Salad

1. Lightly salt the cucumber and drain in a colander for 30 minutes.

2. In a mixing bowl, combine the lime juice and sugar, stirring until dissolved. Mash garlic into the mixture.

3. In a large bowl, mix together the cucumbers, papaya, carrots, parsley, mint, and lime zest. Stir in fish sauce, and season to taste.

1 teaspoon salt

2 English cucumbers, peeled and seeded and thinly sliced or julienned

Juice from 4 large limes

2 teaspoons sugar

4 garlic cloves, chopped

2 green papayas, peeled, seeded, and thinly sliced or julienned

4 carrots, peeled and thinly sliced or julienned

2 tablespoons chopped flat-leaf parsley

2 tablespoons chopped fresh mint

Zest from 4 limes

1 tablespoon nam pla (Thai fish sauce)

Coarse salt and freshly ground black pepper, to taste

Thai Pesto

1. Combine first 5 ingredients in food processor; process to a paste.

2. Drizzle in oil to form a pesto consistency.

3. Add nuts and pulse until chopped.

WHAT TO DRINK: Pour crisp Chateau Ste. Michelle Riesling, Washington, with hints of ripe peaches, apples, and melon that lift this dish's complex flavors.

1 cup fresh basil leaves

2 cups cilantro leaves

¼ cup fresh mint

2 tablespoons fresh chopped ginger

2 garlic cloves

4 tablespoons light oil or fragrant nut oil (like macadamia nut oil)

3 tablespoons macadamia nuts, toasted

Westphalian Potato Pancakes with Smoked Salmon and Chive Sour Cream

BIERGARTEN ❊ *EPCOT* ❊ WALT DISNEY WORLD RESORT

SERVES 4

1 pound Idaho potatoes, peeled

1 small onion

2 eggs

3 tablespoons flour

Coarse salt, to taste

Vegetable oil for frying

4 slices smoked salmon

½ cup Chive Sour Cream (*recipe follows*)

1. Coarsely grate potatoes and onion.
2. In a large bowl, stir together potatoes, onion, eggs, and flour; season with salt, to taste.
3. Heat 3 tablespoons vegetable oil in a skillet. When hot enough to sputter a drop of water, add the potatoes using a tablespoon to place in skillet. Flatten with a spatula and fry about 5 minutes, until golden on the bottom. Turn and fry on the second side. Repeat until all mixture is used, adding oil as needed.
4. Drain on paper towels. To serve, place potato pancake on a small serving plate; top with a slice of smoked salmon; place another potato pancake on top of the salmon, and drizzle with chive sour cream.

Chive Sour Cream

½ cup sour cream

1 bundle chives, finely chopped (at least 2 tablespoons)

Coarse salt and freshly ground black pepper, to taste

Juice from 1 lemon, optional

Mix all ingredients together in a small bowl.

Fettuccine Alfredo

L'ORIGINALE ALFREDO DI ROMA RISTORANTE ❊ *EPCOT* ❊ WALT DISNEY WORLD RESORT

SERVES 4

1. With an electric mixer, beat 2 sticks butter and grated Parmesan cheese until creamy.

2. Cook fettuccine according to package directions. Drain pasta, reserving ½ cup water.

3. Return fettuccine to pot. Toss with salt, cheese mixture, and ¼ cup of the reserved water until all strands are coated. (Add more reserved water as needed to make a smooth, creamy sauce.)

4. Garnish with fresh Parmesan.

WHAT TO DRINK: Masi Campofioran Ripasso, Veneto, stands up to the richness of this Italian favorite.

1 cup (2 sticks) butter, softened

½ pound Parmesan cheese, grated

1 pound fettuccine (preferably fresh)

½ teaspoon salt

Freshly grated Parmesan cheese, for garnish

Bouillabaisse Provençale

BISTRO DE PARIS ❇ *EPCOT* ❇ WALT DISNEY WORLD RESORT

- ½ cup olive oil
- 2 garlic cloves, minced
- 1 shallot, sliced
- 1 bay leaf
- 2 cups peeled fresh tomatoes
- 2 cups Fish Stock (*recipe follows*)
- 1 cup dry white wine
- ½ teaspoon fennel seeds
- ⅛ teaspoon saffron
- 1 teaspoon coarse salt
- ¼ teaspoon freshly ground black pepper
- 2 tablespoons chopped parsley
- 2 raw lobster tails, without the shell, cut in 4 pieces
- 1 pound cod, cut in 1½-inch pieces
- 1 pound sea bass, cut in 1½-inch pieces
- 1 pound snapper, cut in 1½-inch pieces
- 12 medium shrimp
- 8 clams
- 8 mussels
- 8 slices crusty bread
- 8 teaspoons Aïoli (*recipe follows*)

SERVES 8

1. Heat oil in large stockpot over medium-high heat. Add garlic and shallot, and cook until shallots are tender.

2. Add bay leaf, tomatoes, fish stock, wine, fennel seeds, saffron, salt, pepper, and parsley; bring to a boil, reduce heat, and simmer for 20 minutes, stirring occasionally.

3. Ten minutes before serving, add lobster, cod, sea bass, and snapper, and cook 5 minutes. Add shellfish and cook 5 more minutes, or until shells open.

4. Ladle into wide serving bowls, and serve with crusty bread and a dollop of aïoli.

Aïoli

1. Using a large, heavy knife or mortar and pestle, mince and mash garlic to a paste with a pinch of salt.

2. Whisk together egg yolk, lemon juice, and mustard in a bowl.

3. Combine two oils and add, a few drops at a time, to yolk mixture, whisking constantly, until thoroughly mixed. (If mixture separates, stop adding oil and continue whisking until mixture comes together, then resume adding oil.)

4. Whisk in garlic paste and season with salt and pepper. If aioli is too thick, whisk in 1 or 2 drops of water. Chill, covered, until ready to use. Can be chilled up to 2 days.

2 garlic cloves

Pinch salt

1 large egg yolk

2 teaspoons fresh lemon juice

½ teaspoon Dijon mustard

¼ cup extra-virgin olive oil

3 tablespoons vegetable oil

Coarse salt and freshly ground pepper, to taste

Fish Stock

1. Heat oil in a 5-quart heavy pot over moderately high heat until hot but not smoking, then sauté onion, carrots, and celery, stirring occasionally for 6 to 8 minutes, until golden.

2. Add fish bones and trimmings, water, vinegar, peppercorns, and salt, and bring to a boil, skimming froth, then reduce heat and simmer, uncovered, 30 minutes.

3. Pour stock through a fine-mesh sieve into a large bowl, discarding solids. If using stock right away, skim off and discard any fat. If not, cool stock completely, uncovered, before skimming fat (it will be easier to remove when cool), then chill, covered.

Cooks' notes: Fish stock keeps 1 week covered and chilled, or 3 months frozen.

What to drink: From the south of France, Chateau La Marque Rose, Costières de Nîmes, is perfect for sipping with this Provence-inspired dish.

2 tablespoons olive oil

1 large onion, chopped

2 carrots, chopped

2 celery ribs, chopped

2 pounds bones and trimmings of white fish such as sole, flounder, and whiting, chopped (ask your fish market one day ahead to save the bones)

8 cups water

2 tablespoons white-wine vinegar

4 whole black peppercorns

2 teaspoons salt

Pork Loin with XO Sauce

NINE DRAGONS ❋ *EPCOT* ❋ WALT DISNEY WORLD RESORT

SERVES 4 TO 6

1. In a large glass bowl, mix together first 8 ingredients. Add pork, cover, and marinate in refrigerator for at least 30 minutes.

2. Make XO Sauce and keep warm.

3. Heat vegetable oil in a large frying pan, then over medium-high heat, sauté pork slices about 5 to 7 minutes, until golden brown, turning once.

4. To serve, pour XO Sauce over pork. Garnish with green onions.

5. Serve immediately with steamed rice and stir-fried green beans (both can be made ahead of time and kept warm).

XO Sauce

1. In a small bowl, dissolve 3 tablespoons cornstarch in the chicken broth. Set aside.

2. For XO Sauce, in another small bowl, stir together soy sauce, oyster sauce, and XO paste. Set aside.

3. Heat the vegetable oil in a small saucepan; add garlic and sauté until golden. Stir in XO sauce from Step 2, then cooking wine.

4. Gradually stir in the chicken bouillon, sugar, white pepper, and sesame oil.

5. Once mixture begins to bubble, stir in cornstarch mixture. (You may need to add water for desired consistency.)

6. Strain, set aside, and keep warm.

WHAT TO DRINK: The dry Trimbach Gewurztraminer, Alsace is full-bodied with lovely exotic flavors of spiced pear, lychee nuts, and rose petals.

1½ teaspoons salt

1½ teaspoons dried chicken base

1 tablespoon Asian cooking wine

1 tablespoon cornstarch

1 tablespoon flour

1 egg

1 tablespoon sesame oil

White pepper, to taste

1 pound boneless pork loin, cut in ½-inch-thick slices

XO Sauce (*recipe follows*)

3 tablespoons vegetable oil

Green onions, sliced, for garnish

3 tablespoons cornstarch

1½ teaspoons chicken bouillon

3 teaspoons soy sauce

1½ teaspoons oyster sauce

2 tablespoons XO paste (available in Asian markets)

2 tablespoons vegetable oil

1 tablespoon chopped garlic

2 tablespoons Asian cooking wine

1 tablespoon chicken bouillon

1 tablespoon sugar

White pepper, to taste

1 tablespoon sesame oil

⅔ cup of water, to thin sauce if needed

Chicken Tajine
with Preserved Lemon
and Olives

RESTAURANT MARRAKESH ✳ *EPCOT* ✳ WALT DISNEY WORLD RESORT

SERVES 2

1. Wash and dry chicken and cut into quarters.

2. In a large saucepan, heat the olive oil and sauté the onions. Add chicken, breast side down, and brown.

3. Add parsley, ginger, garlic, white pepper, and saffron. Cook for 10 minutes, turning the chicken occasionally.

4. Add water and bring to a boil. Reduce heat and simmer, covered, for 45 minutes, or until chicken is cooked. Remove chicken and place on a tajine or serving dish.

5. Reduce the sauce for 5 minutes, then add olives and preserved lemon.

6. Add sauce to chicken and serve immediately.

WHAT TO DRINK: Try Spice Route Chenin Blanc, Alsace, a delightful white wine with flavors of ripe melon, pears, lemon citrus, and honey blossom.

2½-pound chicken

¼ cup olive oil

2 large onions, chopped

1 bunch fresh parsley, finely chopped

1 teaspoon chopped fresh ginger

1 teaspoon fresh chopped garlic

½ teaspoon white pepper

1 pinch saffron

2 cups water

½ cup green and/or black olives, pitted

2 preserved lemons, sliced (available at specialty markets)

Guinness Stew

SERVES 6 TO 8

2 pounds sirloin steak,
cut into 1-inch cubes

½ cup all-purpose flour

2 tablespoons olive oil

2 bay leaves

1 large clove garlic, chopped

1 cup diced yellow onion

½ cup diced carrots

1 tablespoon
chopped fresh thyme

1 tablespoon
chopped fresh rosemary

¼ teaspoon red chili flakes

1 cup Guinness Stout

Coarse salt and freshly ground
pepper, to taste

1 quart (4 cups) beef broth

1. Place steak and flour in a plastic bag; seal bag and shake vigorously to coat.

2. Heat oil in a large, heavy-bottomed stockpot; add steak and cook over medium-high heat until browned, stirring occasionally. Reserve remaining flour in bag.

3. Add bay leaves, garlic, onions, and carrots, and cook about 5 minutes, until tender. Sprinkle in remaining flour; cook 1 minute, stirring constantly. Add thyme, rosemary, and chili flakes.

4. Slowly stir in Guinness Stout while scraping the bottom of the pan to loosen any particles. Stir until smooth, thickened, and bubbly. Season with salt and pepper. Simmer 10 minutes.

5. Slowly stir in beef broth and bring to a boil. Cover, reduce heat, and simmer 1 hour. Stew will thicken and reduce by at least ⅓. Discard bay leaves before serving.

WHAT TO DRINK: Guinness Stout, of course.

San Angel Inn's Beef Tenderloin in Chili Sauce

SERVES 6

1. Heat oven to broil.

2. Slice pasilla and guajillo chilis in half. Remove and discard stems and ribs. Place on a foil-lined roasting pan.

3. Broil skin side up until skins are blackened. Transfer to a bowl, cover with plastic wrap, and let peppers steam and cool for 15 to 20 minutes. Peel and discard the skins.

4. In a medium-size pot over medium heat, stir together roasted chilis, tomatoes, cloves, and water. Simmer for 10 minutes.

5. Put mixture in a blender, purée, and strain. Set aside and keep warm.

6. In a heavy skillet, heat vegetable oil and sauté beef, poblano chilis, onions, and garlic. Season with pepper and cumin, and cook for 3 minutes, or until beef is done.

7. Add sauce and simmer for 5 minutes. Season with salt, to taste.

8. Serve with rice or warm tortillas

3 pasilla chilis

3 guajillo chilis

2 tomatoes, cut in half

4 whole cloves

2½ cups water

3 tablespoons vegetable oil

2 pounds beef tenderloin, cut in ¾-inch pieces

2 poblano chilis, stems and seeds removed

1 Spanish onion, diced

4 garlic cloves, minced

¼ teaspoon black pepper

¼ teaspoon ground cumin

Coarse salt, to taste

COOKS' NOTES: This recipe uses three fresh chilis, found in Mexican markets and many supermarkets. Pasilla chilis are richly flavored and medium hot; guajillo chilis can be quite hot; while poblanos have a rich flavor that varies from mild to snappy.

WHAT TO DRINK: From Chile, Casillero del Diablo Carmenere, Rapel, matches this beef dish, with bright blackberry and plum fruit flavors.

Thai Noodle Bowl
with Coconut-Crusted Tofu

THE HOLLYWOOD BROWN DERBY ✳ DISNEY-MGM STUDIOS ✳ WALT DISNEY WORLD RESORT

SERVES 4

1 pound yellow Thai noodles
(available at specialty markets)

1 pound package firm tofu

2 tablespoons cornstarch

Tempura Batter (*recipe follows*)

4 tablespoons
shredded coconut

6 tablespoons
vegetable oil, divided

4 small heads baby bok choy

1 cup shiitake mushrooms,
roughly chopped

1 cup fresh snow peas

4 cups Flavored Miso Broth
(*recipe follows*)

4 tablespoons red curry

¼ stalk lemon grass,
thinly sliced lengthwise

1 tablespoon green onions,
sliced diagonally

1. Cook Thai noodles al dente according to package directions and set aside.

2. Drain tofu and cut into 4 equal squares or triangles. Lightly roll in cornstarch, then tempura batter, then coconut.

3. Heat 4 tablespoons vegetable oil in a skillet over medium-high heat; fry tofu until coconut is golden brown, turning once. Remove from pan, drain on paper towels, and keep warm.

4. In a separate pan with 2 tablespoons oil, stir-fry the bok choy, shiitake mushrooms, and snow peas until crisp-tender, about 2–3 minutes. Add miso broth, scraping particles from bottom. Stir in red curry.

5. Divide noodles and vegetable-miso broth evenly among 4 serving bowls.

6. Top each with one piece of tofu.

7. Garnish with lemon grass and green onions and serve immediately.

Tempura Batter

¼ cup all-purpose flour

1 tablespoon cornstarch

1 teaspoon baking powder

½ teaspoon coarse salt

¼ cup water

In a bowl, whisk together flour, cornstarch, baking powder, and salt. Slowly whisk in water until smooth.

Flavored Miso Broth

Place all ingredients in a pot and bring to a slow simmer for 1 hour. Strain and serve.

2 quarts (8 cups) water

¼ fresh jalapeño pepper, seeded and roughly chopped

2 tablespoons rice wine vinegar

1 teaspoon roughly chopped lemon grass

1 teaspoon smashed garlic

¼ cup miso

2 tablespoons soy sauce

1 teaspoon fresh ginger root, unpeeled and roughly chopped

1 teaspoon sesame oil

¾ cup tomato juice

RECONNECT. *Whether friends across the street or families across the globe, we delight*  *in the simple ritual of gathering at the dinner table. A delicious dish can start a rich conversation: a fragrant bowl of Boma's Curry Butternut Soup evokes tales of world travels; a basket of crisp Hush*

MAGICALGATHERINGS

Puppies brings back memories of a trip to Disneyland New Orleans Square; French Toast with Fresh Berries and Mascarpone Cream from Tony's Town Square might just start a new family tradition. Celebrate cherished memories. Enjoy being together. Food is sustenance, but what really nourishes us is our connection to those around us.

Curry Butternut Soup

SERVES 6

1. Melt butter in a large stockpot over medium-high heat. Add onions and garlic and cook about 5 minutes, until tender.

2. Add cumin, coriander, lemon juice, and curry paste.

3. Add squash and vegetable stock. Simmer about 20 minutes, or until squash is easily pierced with a fork.

4. Purée soup in batches until smooth. Add salt and pepper to taste.

5. Return to heat and add milk and sour cream. Do not boil.

6. Adjust seasoning, if necessary. Garnish with cilantro if desired, and serve immediately.

WHAT TO DRINK: Kanu Chenin Blanc, Stellenbosch has a bright melon and crisp pear flavors that balance the soup's spicy richness.

2 tablespoons butter

1 medium onion, chopped

1 clove garlic, chopped

1 teaspoon ground cumin

1 teaspoon ground coriander

Juice of 2 fresh lemons

2 teaspoons
Thai red curry paste
(available in specialty markets)

1 pound butternut squash,
peeled, seeded, cut into chunks

2 cups vegetable stock

Coarse salt and freshly ground pepper, to taste

2 cups milk

4 tablespoons sour cream

Cilantro for garnish, optional

Shrimp and Prosciutto Penne Pasta

GRAND FLORIDIAN CAFE ✳ DISNEY'S GRAND FLORIDIAN RESORT & SPA
✳ WALT DISNEY WORLD RESORT

SERVES 4

1 pound penne pasta

2 tablespoons olive oil

1 tablespoon chopped garlic

10 ounces medium-size shrimp

½ cup chopped prosciutto

½ cup white wine

1 cup heavy cream

½ cup shredded fresh
Parmesan cheese

¼ cup chopped basil

¼ cup diced fresh tomatoes

1. Cook pasta according to package directions; drain and keep warm.

2. Warm olive oil in a large skillet. Add the garlic, shrimp, and prosciutto and sauté over medium heat for about 3 minutes, until shrimp are pink, firm, and slightly opaque.

3. Add white wine and simmer for 1 minute.

4. Stir in cream and cheese. Gently fold in cooked pasta.

5. Garnish with basil and tomatoes.

WHAT TO DRINK: Try Rosemount Estate Show Reserve Chardonnay, Australia, with rich flavors of ripe pear and white peach framed with vanilla flavors from toasted oak that combine to perfectly balance this pasta dish.

Goofy's Goofy Lasagna

CHEF MICKEY'S ❋ *DISNEY'S CONTEMPORARY RESORT* ❋ WALT DISNEY WORLD RESORT

SERVES 8

1 tablespoon minced fresh garlic

2 tablespoons cilantro pesto

1 tablespoon
sun-dried tomato pesto

2 tablespoons olive oil

1 teaspoon coarse salt

1/8 teaspoon freshly ground pepper

2 cups thinly sliced zucchini

1 cup diced and seeded tomatoes

1 medium green pepper,
seeded and julienned

1 medium red pepper,
seeded and julienned

1/2 cup chopped frozen spinach,
thawed and squeezed dry

1/4 cup ricotta cheese

2 tablespoons heavy cream

2 tablespoons grated
fresh Parmesan cheese

2 cups grated provolone cheese

2 cups grated mozzarella cheese

3 large chipotle pepper tortillas

1. Preheat oven to 350°F.

2. In a large bowl, mix garlic, 2 pestos, olive oil, salt, and pepper.

3. Stir in zucchini, tomatoes, peppers, and spinach.

4. In another large bowl, stir together ricotta cheese, heavy cream, and Parmesan cheese. Add the provolone and mozzarella, and mix well.

5. Spray bottom of a 12-inch round casserole baking dish with nonstick cooking spray.

6. Place one of the tortillas in bottom of dish. Spread one-third of cheese mixture over the tortilla. Follow with one-half of the vegetable mixture.

7. Repeat procedure with second tortilla, cheese, and vegetables.

8. Place third tortilla on top and spread with remaining cheese. Cover with foil (spray nonshiny side of foil with nonstick cooking spray to keep from sticking).

9. Bake 40 minutes; remove foil and brown an additional 15 minutes, or until hot and bubbly.

10. Let stand 15 minutes, before cutting. Slice into 8 wedges.

COOKS' NOTES: If you can't find cilantro pesto, use Goofy's Goofy Cilantro Pesto (*recipe follows*)

WHAT TO DRINK: Pour Tiziano Chianti DOCG, Tuscany, with the flavor of bing cherries and a sharp acidity that will delightfully match the lasagna.

Goofy's Goofy Cilantro Pesto

Pulse the first four ingredients in a food processor until blended. With the motor running, add just enough olive oil to make a paste.

2 tablespoons pine nuts, toasted

1 clove garlic

½ bunch cilantro

3 tablespoons grated Parmesan cheese

Olive oil

Crystal Palace Adobo Pulled Pork

THE CRYSTAL PALACE ✳ MAGIC KINGDOM PARK ✳ WALT DISNEY WORLD RESORT

SERVES 4 TO 6

1. Combine the first 10 ingredients in a heavy-duty, zip-top plastic bag. Add pork; seal bag, and chill 24 hours, turning occasionally.

2. When ready to bake, preheat oven for at least 15 minutes to 400°F.

3. Place pork in an ovenproof dish, pour marinade over pork, and add water. Bake uncovered for 30 minutes. Reduce oven temperature 300°F, cover, and cook for about 3 more hours.

4. Remove from oven and let stand for 10 minutes. To serve, shred pork and mix with its juices.

Juice of 1 orange

Juice of 2 limes

1 tablespoon Dijon mustard

3 tablespoons minced fresh garlic

1 cup extra-virgin olive oil

2 tablespoons coarse salt

1½ teaspoons freshly ground black pepper

1½ teaspoons ground cumin

2 tablespoons sugar

2 tablespoons canned chipotle peppers, chopped

6-pound pork roast, leg, or shoulder

1 cup water

Roasted Chicken Linguine

SHUTTERS RESTAURANT ✸ DISNEY'S VERO BEACH RESORT

SERVES 4 TO 6

1. Pull chicken from bones and tear into bite-sized pieces. Set aside.

2. Cook linguine according to package directions. Drain, rinse with cold water, and set aside.

3. Heat olive oil in a large skillet over medium heat. Add garlic and stir for 30 seconds (don't let it burn). Add sun-dried tomatoes and pine nuts, stirring until nuts are lightly browned.

4. Add chicken, spinach, and feta and goat cheeses, stirring until creamy.

5. Add linguine and heat through. Add basil, then season with salt and pepper.

6. Garnish with fresh Parmesan cheese.

WHAT TO DRINK: Match this dish with Chateau de Montfort Vouvray, Loire, with fresh mineral scents of peaches, lime, melon, and honey.

2½- to 3-pound chicken, roasted (or from the deli)

1 pound dry linguine

1 cup extra-virgin olive oil

2 tablespoons chopped fresh garlic

3 tablespoons chopped sun-dried tomatoes

2 tablespoons pine nuts

½ 10-ounce bag of prewashed fresh spinach

½ cup feta cheese, crumbled

½ cup goat cheese

½ bunch fresh basil, chopped

Coarse salt and freshly ground black pepper, to taste

Fresh Parmesan cheese, shredded for garnish

Loaded Baked Potato Soup

CARNATION CAFÉ ❉ *DISNEYLAND PARK* ❉ DISNEYLAND RESORT

SERVES 6

1 pound bacon,
roughly chopped

1 medium yellow onion, diced

1 large carrot,
peeled and diced

¾ cup diced celery

4 large russet potatoes,
peeled and diced

4 medium red potatoes, diced

¼ cup flour

2 cups chicken
or vegetable stock

Coarse salt and freshly ground
pepper, to taste

4 cups heavy cream

OPTIONAL GARNISHES:
chopped chives, bacon bits,
sour cream, shredded cheddar
and Monterey Jack cheeses

1. In a 6- to 8-quart stockpot over medium heat, fry bacon until crisp.

2. Remove bacon and drain on paper towels (reserve half for garnish). In the bacon fat, cook onions, carrots, and celery until the onions are translucent. Add potatoes and cook for 4 minutes, stirring occasionally.

3. Sprinkle in flour and stir constantly over low heat about 5 to 7 minutes until the mixture has thickened slightly. Add stock and half of the bacon. Season with salt and pepper.

4. Over medium-high heat, bring the soup to a simmer and cook for 25 minutes, or until the potatoes are soft. Mash some of the potatoes for thicker, creamier texture. Add cream and simmer for 5 minutes.

5. Adjust thickness by adding water or stock. Soup should have a creamy consistency.

6. Season to taste, and garnish with toppings, if desired.

COOKS' NOTES: Soak diced potatoes in cold water until ready to use to keep them from turning brown. To make bacon easier to chop, lightly freeze.

WHAT TO DRINK: Pour Ferrari-Carano Merlot, Sonoma County to match this rich soup. Black cherry aromas and flavors of ripe black plums with spicy oak stand up to the creamy soup.

Disneyland Hush Puppies

BLUE BAYOU RESTAURANT ✳ *DISNEYLAND PARK* ✳ DISNEYLAND RESORT

MAKES 2 ½ DOZEN

1. In a large mixing bowl, combine all ingredients except the egg, milk, and oil.

2. In a separate bowl, mix together egg and milk. Using a deep pot, preheat oil for frying to 350°F.

3. Add the dry ingredients to the egg mixture. Do not let the batter sit longer than 15 minutes.

4. Use two teaspoons and carefully spoon a ball about the size of a large olive. Fry in the oil until golden brown, about 3 to 4 minutes, turning once. Drain on paper towels and serve at once.

½ cup plus 1 tablespoon of flour

1 cup yellow cornmeal

1 tablespoon finely diced shallot

2 heaping tablespoons cooked and finely chopped bacon

1½ teaspoons finely chopped parsley

3 heaping tablespoons white sweet corn

1¼ teaspoons baking powder

1 teaspoon sugar

1½ teaspoon salt

½ teaspoon black pepper

1 egg

¾ cup milk

4 cups corn oil or shortening

French Toast with Fresh Berries and Mascarpone Cream

TONY'S TOWN SQUARE RESTAURANT ✳ *MAGIC KINGDOM PARK*
✳ WALT DISNEY WORLD RESORT

SERVES 8

6 whole eggs

4 cups whole milk

1 teaspoon vanilla extract

8 pieces of thick-cut white bread or sourdough

½ cup mascarpone cheese, softened

½ cup confectioners' sugar

1 cup heavy cream

½ cup fresh strawberries, hulled and halved

½ cup fresh blueberries

1 tablespoon fresh orange zest

1. In a large bowl, whisk together eggs, milk, and vanilla.

2. Evenly coat bread, absorbing all the mixture.

3. On a nonstick griddle, grill bread about 2 minutes on each side, or until golden brown. Keep warm in oven and cook in batches.

4. In a bowl, combine mascarpone, confectioners' sugar, and cream to the consistency of melted ice cream. Adjust with a few extra tablespoons of heavy cream if needed.

5. Cut French toast pieces diagonally; top with strawberries and blueberries, then drizzle with mascarpone cream. Sprinkle with orange zest and serve immediately.

COOKS' NOTE: You can serve with traditional maple syrup, but it's not necessary—the mascarpone cream and fresh berries add sweetness.

FRUIT, PASTA, PIZZA . . . forget hot dogs and hamburgers, some foods go straight to the head of the class. Dinner takes on a whole new appeal when little ones get to play with their food: let them build their own salad, dip fresh fruit in creamy yogurt, or scoop their own salsa with a

FOOD**FORKIDS**

*baked wedge of tortilla. Veggies get a makeover with a touch of brown sugar. Even fish gets a nod when it's served with a **sweet**, fresh pineapple relish. When it comes to food, variety—flavor, color, and texture—is the spice of life. View healthy eating as a great family adventure!*

Mickey's Favorite Chicken Parmesan

VARIOUS RESTAURANTS ✻ WALT DISNEY WORLD RESORT

SERVES 4

2 cups dried whole-grain pasta

1 tablespoon olive oil

4 boneless, skinless chicken breasts, each cut into 3 equal pieces

3½ cups favorite marinara sauce

3 cups fresh broccoli, cut in bite-size pieces

1½ cups fresh baby carrots

⅛ teaspoon salt, or to taste

1¼ cups shredded mozzarella cheese

1. Cook pasta according to package directions. Drain and keep warm.

2. While pasta is cooking, heat a nonstick sauté pan over medium-high heat. Brown chicken in olive oil about 6 to 8 minutes, until done. Keep warm.

3. In a saucepan over medium heat, bring marinara sauce to a simmer.

4. Steam the broccoli and carrots about 8 to 10 minutes, until cooked but slightly firm. Season with salt to taste.

5. Mix together warm pasta with 1½ cups of marinara sauce. Mix in 1 cup of mozzarella.

6. Serve with chicken and steamed vegetables, evenly divided on 4 plates. Top with remaining marinara and cheese.

COOKS' NOTES: For a "complete" meal that includes one serving from each of the five food groups, pair this dish with the fruit salad on page 154.

Just Dip It

SERVES 4

Divide evenly on 4 serving plates: vegetables with ranch dressing, fruit with yogurt, and crackers with chicken salad.

12 2-inch-long
peeled baby carrots

12 2-inch-long celery sticks

12 ¼-inch-thick sliced
cucumber wheels

12 red grape tomatoes

8 tablespoons
fat-free ranch dressing

12 peeled, cored,
1-inch pineapple cubes

12 strawberries, cleaned,
hulled, and cut into halves

2 Granny Smith apples,
cut in halves, halves cut into
4 slices lengthwise

4 6-ounce containers light
strawberry yogurt

Wheat crackers

1⅓ cups Nothing-but-
Chicken Salad
(*recipe follows*)

Nothing-but-Chicken Salad

SERVES 4

Finely chop chicken, then stir in mayonnaise and salt. Refrigerate until serving.

2 cups cooked chicken meat

½ cup mayonnaise

½ teaspoon coarse salt

Totally Tasty Tofu

VARIOUS RESTAURANTS ❇ WALT DISNEY WORLD RESORT

SERVES 4

8 slices fresh pineapple, peeled, cored and cut into half-inch "moon" slices

1 teaspoon light olive oil

Marinated Tofu (*recipe follows*)

¼ cup vegetable broth

2 cups Power Pilaf (*recipe follows*)

3 cups steamed broccoli

1½ cups steamed baby carrots

1. Preheat a nonstick sauté pan over medium-high heat. Sear pineapple slices on each side until golden brown. Remove from pan and keep warm.
2. Reduce heat to medium and wipe pan clean. Add olive oil and sear tofu on all sides until golden brown.
3. Add vegetable broth, cover, and remove from heat.
4. Serve pilaf, tofu, and steamed vegetables topped with seared pineapple slices.

Marinated Tofu

1 pound firm tofu

2 tablespoons olive oil

⅓ cup low-sodium soy sauce

1 teaspoon minced garlic

1 teaspoon minced peeled fresh ginger

1 teaspoon chopped cilantro

1. Drain tofu. On a small plate, wrap tofu in paper towels, then cover with another small plate. Refrigerate for 1 hour to let drain.
2. Mix together the remaining ingredients. Seal tofu in a plastic bag with the marinade and refrigerate for 1 hour, turning occasionally.

Power Pilaf

1. Heat a saucepan over medium-high heat. Add olive oil, garlic, onions, celery, and carrots and cook 1 minute.

2. Stir in rice and quinoa. Add vegetable broth; cover and reduce heat to low.

3. Cook for 25 minutes, or until all liquid has been absorbed.

4. Remove from heat, add red and green peppers, and season with salt. Serve immediately.

1 tablespoon light olive oil

½ teaspoon minced fresh garlic

2 tablespoons finely diced red onion

2 tablespoons finely chopped celery

2 tablespoons finely chopped carrot

½ cup brown rice

¼ cup quinoa

1½ cups vegetable broth

1 tablespoon finely chopped red pepper

1 tablespoon finely chopped green pepper

½ teaspoon coarse salt

Yummy Pita Pizza

VARIOUS RESTAURANTS ❋ WALT DISNEY WORLD RESORT

SERVES 4

4 whole-wheat
"pocketless" pitas

1 cup favorite pizza sauce

1¾ cups grated
mozzarella cheese

1½ cups chopped cooked
chicken breast

So Sweet Brown Sugar Apples
(*recipe follows*)

1. Preheat oven to 350°F.

2. Place pitas on a parchment paper–lined baking pan.

3. Spread ¼ cup pizza sauce on top of each pita.
    Top with cheese, then chicken breast.

4. Bake 10–12 minutes, or until cheese is melted.

5. Serve with So Sweet Brown Sugar Apples.

So Sweet Brown Sugar Apples

MAKES 3 CUPS

4 Granny Smith apples, halved,
cored, sliced thin lengthwise

½ cup light brown sugar

1 teaspoon ground cinnamon

Place ingredients in a small bowl and toss to fully coat apples. Serve cold.

COOKS' NOTES: Add a small green salad to the pizza and apples, and you'll have a serving from each of the five food groups.

Oodles of Noodles Beef 'N Mac

VARIOUS RESTAURANTS ✳ WALT DISNEY WORLD RESORT

SERVES 4

2 cup dried whole-grain macaroni

½ pound lean ground beef

1½ cups favorite marinara sauce

1½ cups fresh green beans, snipped and broken into 2-inch pieces

1½ cups fresh baby carrots, peeled

⅛ teaspoon salt, or to taste

1½ cups shredded mozzarella cheese, divided

Tooty Fruity Salad (*recipe follows*)

1. Cook macaroni according to package directions. Drain and keep warm.

2. While pasta is cooking, heat a nonstick sauté pan over medium-high heat and brown ground beef, breaking into small pieces. Cook for about 4 to 5 minutes, until beef is browned. Drain off excess fat.

3. Reduce heat to medium-low and add the marinara sauce.

4. While sauce is simmering, steam green beans and carrots about 8 to 10 minutes, until slightly firm. Season to taste.

5. Mix macaroni into sauce, then stir in 1 cup of mozzarella. To serve, sprinkle with remaining mozzarella and serve vegetables on the side.

6. Serve with Tooty Fruity Salad.

Tooty Fruity Salad

SERVES 4

¾ cup peeled, seeded and ½-inch cubes of cantaloupe

¾ cup peeled, seeded and ½-inch cubes of honeydew melon

¾ cup red grapes

¾ cup peeled, cored and ½-inch cubes of pineapple

2 tablespoons shredded sweetened coconut

In a small bowl, mix together fruit. Sprinkle with shredded coconut. Chill before serving.

"Deconstructed" Quesadilla

VARIOUS RESTAURANTS ❋ WALT DISNEY WORLD RESORT

2 cups shredded
iceberg lettuce

1 cup Oh-So-Fresh
Tomato Salsa (*recipe follows*)

½ cup sour cream

Baked Wedgies Wedges
(*recipe follows*)

3 cups Very Veggie Bean and
Corn Dip (*recipe follows*)

½ cup shredded
light cheddar cheese

SERVES 4

1.   Arrange lettuce, salsa, sour cream, and baked tortilla chips onto 4 plates.

2.   Ladle warm bean and corn dip into 4 small bowls and top each with
     2 tablespoons of grated cheese.

Baked Wedgies Wedges

SERVES 4

1.   Preheat oven to 350°F.

2.   Stack tortillas on top of each other and cut into 8 wedges.

3.   Spread wedges in a single layer on a parchment paper–lined baking pan.

4.   Bake for 10 minutes, or until crisp. Cool to room temperature.

4 6-inch whole-wheat tortillas

Oh-So-Fresh Tomato Salsa

MAKES 1 CUP

Mix all of the ingredients together in a small bowl.

¾ cup chopped tomatoes

¼ cup minced red onion

1 teaspoon fresh lemon juice

1 teaspoon
finely chopped cilantro

½ teaspoon coarse salt

Very Veggie Bean and Corn Dip

MAKES 3 CUPS

1.   In a saucepan over medium heat, stir beans, corn, and vegetable broth
     until simmering and smooth.

2.   Add grated cheese and continue stirring until cheese melts. Keep warm.

1 16-ounce can refried beans

1½ cups corn kernels

¼ cup vegetable broth

1 cup grated
light cheddar cheese

COOKS' NOTES: For dessert, serve the So Sweet Brown Sugar Apples on page 152.

Groovy Grilled Mahi Mahi with Caramelized Pineapple Relish

VARIOUS RESTAURANTS ❋ WALT DISNEY WORLD RESORT

SERVES 4

½ cup peeled, cored, chopped pineapple

¼ cup finely chopped green bell pepper

¼ cup finely chopped red bell pepper

¼ teaspoon coarse salt

1 pound boneless, skinless mahi mahi fillet, cut into 4 pieces

1 tablespoon light olive oil

Belle's Brown Sugar Sweet Potatoes (*recipe follows*)

1. Heat a sauté pan over medium-high heat. Add pineapple and toss until natural sugars in pineapple are a light brown or caramel color.
2. Remove from heat and toss the pineapple with peppers and salt. Keep warm.
3. Coat fish with olive oil and grill over medium-high heat until done, about 3 minutes each side, turning once.
4. To serve, top fish with warm pineapple relish, and serve with Belle's Brown Sugar Sweet Potatoes.

Belle's Brown Sugar Sweet Potatoes

SERVES 4

1 pound sweet potatoes

2 teaspoons light olive oil

2 tablespoons light brown sugar

¼ teaspoon coarse salt

1. Preheat oven to 400°F.
2. Wash and scrub the sweet potatoes, then cut into ½-inch-by-4-inch wedges.
3. In a mixing bowl combine oil, brown sugar, and salt.
4. Add potatoes to mixing bowl and toss to fully coat potatoes.
5. Arrange coated sweet potatoes on a parchment paper–lined baking pan in a single layer.
6. Bake 10 to 15 minutes, until brown and crispy.

COOKS' NOTES: For a serving from each of the five food groups, finish this meal with the fruit salad on page 154.

INDULGE. Vacation is time for sleeping late, sipping an afternoon cocktail, enjoying a treat from the sweeter side of life. A slice of Peanut Butter Cake or Apple-Caramel Pie. A scoop

DESSERT

of dense Raspberry Gelato. Delectable Chocolate "Lava" Cake. There are plenty of contenders for the favorite Disney dessert, from simple recipes that can be whipped up in minutes to a few that are works of art. Like vacation, luscious *desserts* aren't for every day, *but* sometimes memories can call for a little sugar in the kitchen. Tie on an apron, make something delicious, and enjoy a sensory getaway.

Peanut Butter Pie

DISNEY WONDER & DISNEY MAGIC ✱ *DISNEY CRUISE LINE*

SERVES 8

1½ cups creamy peanut butter

8 ounces cream cheese, softened

¾ cup sugar

2 tablespoons butter, melted

1 cup heavy cream, whipped stiff

1 baked 8-inch pie shell

1. With an electric mixer, blend the peanut butter and cream cheese until smooth.

2. Add the melted butter to peanut butter mixture, then fold in whipped cream.

3. Pour into the baked pie shell and refrigerate for 1 hour.

4. Glaze with Ganache if desired.

Ganache

½ cup heavy cream

4 ounces dark chocolate, chopped

1. In a saucepan over medium heat, bring the cream to a boil. Remove from heat and fold in chocolate until no streaks of white remain.

2. Cool until lukewarm, then glaze cake. Refrigerate for at least 2 hours before serving.

COOKS' NOTES: Ganache is a fancy word for a rich icing of semisweet chocolate and whipping cream.

No-Sugar-Added Cheesecake

BOARDWALK BAKERY ❇ *DISNEY'S BOARDWALK RESORT* ❇ WALT DISNEY WORLD RESORT

MAKES ONE 9-INCH CHEESECAKE

1¼ cups sugar-free vanilla wafer cookies, crushed

4 tablespoons butter, melted

4 tablespoons sugar-free sweetener

2 tablespoons cornstarch

24 oz (3 8-ounce packages) cream cheese, softened

3 eggs

1 egg white

½ cup sour cream

1½ teaspoons fresh lemon juice

1 teaspoon vanilla extract

1. Preheat oven to 375°F.
2. In a mixing bowl, combine cookie crumbs and butter. Press into the bottom of a 9-inch round pan (a springform pan works well).
3. Bake for 7 to 8 minutes. Allow to cool completely.
4. Reduce oven temperature to 325°F.
5. In a large mixing bowl, sift together sweetener and cornstarch. Add cream cheese, then beat at low speed with an electric mixer until creamy.
6. Add eggs, egg white, and sour cream; beat at low speed for 1 minute. Stop the mixer and scrape the sides of the bowl with a spatula; add the lemon juice and vanilla extract, beating 1 more minute.
7. Pour into prepared crust. Bake at 325°F for 45 to 50 minutes, or until firm and golden around the edges but still slightly moist in the center. Let cool thoroughly.

COOKS' NOTES: To slice, dip a knife into hot water and then dry it before cutting. Top with favorite seasonal berries or no-sugar-added preserves.

Chocolate Lava Cake

CALIFORNIA GRILL ✱ *DISNEY'S CONTEMPORARY RESORT* ✱ WALT DISNEY WORLD RESORT

SERVES 6

8 1-ounce squares semisweet chocolate, chopped, or 1 cup semisweet chocolate chips

1 cup (2 sticks) of butter

5 egg yolks

4 whole eggs

¾ cup sugar

⅓ cup all-purpose flour

1. Preheat oven to 375°F. Lightly butter sides of 6 individual (¾ cup) ramekins. Lightly coat with sugar, then shake out excess.

2. Melt chocolate and butter in top of a double boiler set over simmering water. Stir until smooth. Remove from over water and cool 10 minutes.

3. Beat egg yolks and whole eggs together in a large bowl. Add sugar and beat about 2 minutes, until thick and light.

4. Fold in chocolate mixture.

5. Sift flour, then fold into batter, mixing until smooth.

6. Divide batter among prepared cups, filling ¾ full.

7. Place on a baking sheet and bake about 35 to 40 minutes, or until sides of cakes are set and middle is still soft. Do not overbake.

8. Using a small knife, cut around sides of cakes to loosen. Invert onto plates and serve with your favorite ice cream.

COOKS' NOTES: You can also use muffin tins; recipe makes 12. Bake for 15 minutes, or until set and middle is still soft.

WHAT TO DRINK: Guenoc Vintage Port, with sweet flavors of black fruits and vanilla that contrast and complement this decadent dessert.

'Ohana Bread Pudding à la Mode with Bananas Foster Sauce

'OHANA ✳ DISNEY'S POLYNESIAN RESORT
✳ WALT DISNEY WORLD RESORT

SERVES 6 TO 8

1. Preheat oven to 350°F. In a large mixing bowl, whisk together eggs, salt, sugar, cinnamon, nutmeg, and milk.

2. Stir in bread cubes, pineapple, coconut, and raisins, (optional). Pour into a 13x9x2-inch pan coated with cooking spray.

3. Bake for 1 hour and 10 minutes. Remove from oven and let stand for 5 minutes.

4. Serve the hot bread pudding with a scoop of vanilla ice cream and top with warm Bananas Foster Sauce.

5 large eggs

½ teaspoon salt

1½ cups sugar

½ teaspoon cinnamon

⅛ teaspoon ground nutmeg

3 cups whole milk

1 loaf challah bread or egg-style bread, enough to fill 10 cups, cut in ½-inch cubes

1 8-ounce can crushed pineapple, drained

¼ cup sweetened shredded coconut

¼ cup raisins, optional

Vanilla ice cream

Bananas Foster Sauce (*recipe follows*)

Bananas Foster Sauce

1. While the bread pudding is baking, in a medium saucepan over high heat, combine brown sugar, corn syrup, butter, and half of the cream. Bring to a rolling boil.

2. Boil for 10 minutes, then add remaining cream. Boil 1 minute more.

3. Add rum and vanilla. Flambé using a long-stemmed lighter. Let boil until the flame goes out.

4. Reduce to a simmer and stir with a heatproof spatula.

5. Add bananas. Remove from heat and set aside.

1 cup dark brown sugar

½ cup corn syrup

½ cup unsalted butter

1 cup heavy cream, divided

½ cup spiced or dark rum

1 teaspoon vanilla extract

3 bananas, peeled and sliced

Twinkie Tiramisù

EVERYTHING POP! SHOPPING AND DINING ❈ *DISNEY'S POP CENTURY RESORT*
❈ WALT DISNEY WORLD RESORT

SERVES 8 TO 10

12 Twinkies, sliced ½-inch thick

Espresso Syrup (*recipe follows*)

Mascarpone Filling (*recipe follows*)

Cocoa powder, chocolate chips for garnish

1. Place half the Twinkie slices in a single layer in the bottom of a shallow 2-quart baking dish or gratin dish.
2. Drizzle with half of the espresso syrup.
3. Spread with half of the mascarpone filling.
4. Repeat with remaining Twinkies, syrup, and filling.
5. Smooth the top with a metal spatula.
6. Cover with plastic wrap and refrigerate for up to 24 hours before serving.
7. Just before serving, sift cocoa to lightly dust the top of the tiramisù. Sprinkle with chocolate chips.

Espresso Syrup

⅓ cup water

½ cup sugar

⅔ cup strong-brewed espresso coffee

¼ cup Italian or domestic brandy, optional

1. Combine water and sugar in a small saucepan.
2. Bring to a simmer, stirring occasionally to dissolve sugar.
3. Remove from heat, cool, and add coffee and brandy.

Mascarpone Filling

1½ cups heavy cream

⅓ cup sugar

2 teaspoons vanilla extract

1 pound mascarpone cheese, softened

1. Whip cream with sugar and vanilla until soft peaks form.
2. Fold cream into softened mascarpone.

Strawberry Soup

1900 Park Fare ❋ Disney's Grand Floridian Resort & Spa
❋ Walt Disney World Resort

SERVES 6

1. Mix strawberries, cream, sour cream, and yogurt in an electric mixer or blender.

2. Beat at low speed to a smooth consistency.

3. Add sugar, if desired.

4. Chill; stir well before serving.

5. Garnish with fresh strawberry halves.

2½ pounds frozen strawberries, thawed with juice

2 cups heavy cream

¼ cup sour cream

⅓ cup plain yogurt

1 tablespoon sugar, optional

½ pound fresh strawberries, halved for garnish

Apple-Caramel Pie

WHISPERING CANYON CAFE ✳ *DISNEY'S WILDERNESS LODGE* ✳ WALT DISNEY WORLD RESORT

SERVES 12

Crust

½ cup all-purpose flour

13½-ounce package refrigerated sugar cookie dough

1. Preheat oven to 350°F.

2. Coat the bottom and inside of a 9-inch springform pan with nonstick cooking spray.

3. At medium-low speed, beat the flour and the dough until combined.

4. Press sugar cookie dough onto sides and bottom of pan, creating a ¼-inch-thick crust.

Filling

2¼ pounds Granny Smith apples, peeled, cored, cut into half-inch thick slices

½ cup granulated sugar

⅛ cup all-purpose flour

¾ tablespoon chopped candied ginger

¾ teaspoon cinnamon

¾ cup caramel topping

1. In a mixing bowl, toss the apples with sugar, flour, ginger, and cinnamon. Spoon into prepared crust.

2. Spoon on caramel topping.

3. Cover tightly with foil and bake 1 hour.

(Continued)

Crumb Topping

2¼ cups all-purpose flour

½ cup granulated sugar

½ cup dark brown sugar, packed

1½ teaspoons cinnamon

¾ cup (1½ sticks) butter or margarine, melted

1½ teaspoons vanilla extract

¾ cup confectioners' sugar

1. While pie is baking, in a mixing bowl at low speed, combine flour, granulated sugar, brown sugar, and cinnamon.

2. Increase speed to medium; gradually add butter and vanilla, beating until wet crumbs form.

3. Remove pie from oven and uncover.

4. Sprinkle crumb mixture over top of warm pie.

5. Cover exposed edges of crust with aluminum foil to prevent burning.

6. Bake, uncovered, for 20 to 25 minutes or until lightly browned.

7. Cool on a rack and remove sides from the pan.

8. Stir together the confectioners' sugar with enough water to make icing. Transfer to a plastic food storage bag, snip one corner, and drizzle over crumbs. Serve with vanilla ice cream, if desired.

Key Lime Pie

Yacht Club Galley ❊ *Disney's Yacht and Beach Club Resorts* ❊ Walt Disney World Resort

Makes one 9-inch pie

- 1 cup graham cracker crumbs
- 5 tablespoons sugar, divided
- 1 teaspoon cinnamon
- 6 tablespoons (3/4 stick) butter, melted
- 1 14 ounce-can sweetened condensed milk
- 4 egg yolks
- 6 tablespoons Key lime juice
- 1 pint (2 cups) heavy cream

1. Preheat oven to 300°F.
2. In a mixing bowl, combine the graham cracker crumbs, 3 tablespoons of the sugar, and cinnamon. Stir in melted butter; mixture should hold together when squeezed. Press into a 9-inch pie pan.
3. In a bowl, combine milk, egg yolks, and lime juice and mix well. Pour into crust.
4. Bake for 18 to 20 minutes, or until filling is set. Refrigerate for at least 3 hours, until well chilled.
5. Whip the cream and the remaining 2 tablespoons of sugar until stiff peaks form. Top pie with whipped cream and refrigerate until serving time.

Cooks' Notes: True Key lime pie is similar to lemon meringue pie, made with yellowish, very tart Key limes.

What to drink: For something fun, try Florida Orange Groves mango wine, a "pseudo" wine made from mangoes with a very sweet profile—matching the acid and sugary lime essence of this dessert.

Raspberry Gelato

BEACH CLUB MARKETPLACE ✲ *DISNEY'S YACHT AND BEACH CLUB RESORTS* ✲ WALT DISNEY WORLD RESORT

SERVES 4 TO 6

1. In a medium saucepan, heat the sugar and water until the sugar dissolves. Remove from heat and cool.

2. In a blender or food processor, purée the raspberries and strain the seeds. Add the sugar syrup along with the lemon juice and Chambord liqueur. Refrigerate until cold.

3. When cold, pour the mixture into an ice-cream maker. Fill the machine only halfway, as the mixture expands as it freezes.

4. Freeze according to ice-cream maker instructions.

5. As it starts to freeze, add the egg white and freeze until firm. (The egg white will give the gelato a creamy texture.)

COOKS' NOTES: For a festive occasion, serve gelato in a martini glass with fresh mint leaf and a splash of champagne.

1 cup granulated sugar

½ cup spring water

1 cup raspberry purée or 4 cups fresh or frozen raspberries

juice of ½ lemon

2 tablespoons Chambord liqueur

1 egg white

FROM THE EPCOT *International Food and Wine Festival to Artist Point's remarkable collection of Pacific Northwest wines, to more than 17,000 bottles in the Napa Rose cellar, Disney is becoming a premier wine destination. Walt Disney World Resort is the largest single-site purveyor of wine in*

WINE&SPIRITS

the world, with more sommeliers than any other company; Napa Rose at the Grand Californian at Disneyland Resort has more sommeliers than any other restaurant in the world. Beyond wine; cool cocktails, martinis, and mixed drinks add sparkle to vacation time. Now you can get your own party started with these delicious, icy concoctions.

Konk Cooler

❄ *DISNEY CRUISE LINE*

SERVES 1

½ ounce dark rum

¾ ounce light rum

1 ounce passion fruit juice

1 ounce piña colada mix

1 ounce orange juice

Crushed ice

Tropical fruit wedge, for garnish

1. Place the first five ingredients in a cocktail shaker and shake vigorously.

2. Serve in a tall glass filled with crushed ice. Garnish with a wedge of tropical fruit, if desired.

Soul Candy

❄ WALT DISNEY WORLD RESORT

SERVES 1

½ ounce Vincent Van Gogh Dutch Chocolate Vodka

¾ ounce Godiva White Chocolate Liqueur

¾ ounce Godiva Dark Chocolate Liqueur

4 ounces cappuccino

Freshly whipped cream, for garnish

White and dark chocolate shavings, for garnish

Mix the first four ingredients in a warm 12-ounce coffee glass. Garnish with freshly whipped cream and white and dark chocolate shavings.

Big Apple Sunset

❉ WALT DISNEY WORLD RESORT

SERVES 1

In a shaker with ice, mix vodka, schnapps, and sour mix. Strain. Finish with Chambord (do not stir). Serve in a chilled martini glass garnished with apple slices.

1¼ ounces Van Gogh Wild Apple Vodka

¾ ounce sour apple schnapps

½ ounce sour mix

¼ ounce Chambord Raspberry Liqueur

Apple slices, for garnish

Watermelon Mist

❉ WALT DISNEY WORLD RESORT

SERVES 1

Blend the first four ingredients with just enough ice to make a loose slush. Pour into a martini glass and garnish with a wedge of watermelon and fresh mint.

1¼ ounces watermelon schnapps

¾ ounce Midori

2 ounces cranberry juice

Crushed ice

Watermelon wedge, for garnish

Fresh mint, for garnish

ACKNOWLEDGMENTS

For information address Disney Editions,
114 Fifth Avenue, New York, New York 10011-5690.

Printed in Singapore

First Edition
10 9 8 7 6 5 4 3 2

Reinforced binding

Library of Congress Cataloging-in-Publication Data on file.
ISBN: 1-4231-0637-7

At Walt Disney World Resort, a million thanks to Karen Haynes, a true Partner in Excellence, who kept us all on track.

Also to Dieter Hannig, John Blazon, and Judi Rosean in the Food & Beverage office; photographers Debi Harbin, Dianne DeBrosse, Gary Bogdon, and Kent Phillips; Sharon Schifano, Judi William, and Lauren Andersen for recipe testing; Paul Hazzard and Michael Senich in the Disney test kitchen. And to Betsy Singer in Walt Disney World Merchandise.

At Disneyland Resort, Mary Niven, Christopher Maggetti, Bill Rowland, Michael Jordan, Andrew Sutton, Timothy Kopaceski, Janine Ruozi, Toby Holis, Ralph Stuhlmueller, and Karlos Siqueiros.

And from Disney Cruise Line, Antony Wills.

Special thanks to Jon Glick for the beautiful design of this book, and to Wendy Lefkon, our editor at Disney Publishing.